CHRIST IN THE MARGINS

CHRIST IN THE MARGINS

ICONS AND BIOGRAPHIES

by

Robert Lentz

REFLECTIONS

by

Edwina Gateley

Orbis Books
Maryknoll, New York 10545

For Daniel O'Connor,
fellow pilgrim in the margins
—Robert Lentz

For my mother,
who belongs in this book,
and for all the men and women of the Volunteer Missionary Movement (VMM),
who work on the margins throughout the world
—Edwina Gateley

Founded in 1970, Orbis Books endeavors to publish works that enlighten the mind, nourish the spirit, and challenge the conscience. The publishing arm of the Maryknoll Fathers and Brothers, Orbis seeks to explore the global dimensions of the Christian faith and mission, to invite dialogue with diverse cultures and religious traditions, and to serve the cause of reconciliation and peace. The books published reflect the views of their authors and do not represent the official position of the Society. To learn more about Maryknoll and Orbis Books, please visit our website at www.maryknoll.org.

"Tired of Speaking Sweetly," from *The Gift—Poems by Hafiz* translated by Daniel Ladinsky, copyright © 1999 by Daniel Ladinsky. Reprinted by permission of Daniel Ladinsky.

Queries regarding rights and permissions should be addressed to:
Orbis Books, P.O. Box 308, Maryknoll, NY 10545-0308.

Queries regarding the icons should be directed to:
Trinity Stores, PO Box 44944, Eden Prairie, MN 55344-2644
www.trinitystores.com

Manufactured in Spain

Designed by Roberta Savage

Library of Congress Cataloging-in-Publication Data

Lentz, Robert, 1946-
    Christ in the margins/Robert Lentz, Edwina Gateley.
       p.cm.
       ISBN 1-57-75-321-0 (cloth)
    1.   Christian biography. I. Gateley, Edwina. II. Title.
       BR1700.3 .L46 2003
       270'.092'2--dc21

                                        2002153337

Contents

Introduction

This book took shape on a red plastic tablecloth in a diner in Albuquerque, New Mexico. This is where I met the artist Robert Lentz.

The two of us spent hours sharing ideas to bring his vision for this book to reality. Perhaps as we sat together, eyes shining, words tumbling, arms gesticulating, those around us who threw curious glances might well have imagined we were lovers. Indeed we were. We were in love with the Christ we knew danced on the margins of the world, and we were recognizing and naming those who danced with him—Saints Francis and Clare, Steven Biko, Mychal Judge, Elizabeth Cady Stanton, Albert Einstein, Black Elk, Julian of Norwich, Johann Sebastian Bach—and many more. As we spoke of these friends of God we were filled with excitement and joy and we knew that, however long it took, this book must be painted and must be written and must be shared.

For it is time. It is time for all of us who follow Christ to recognize him and to proclaim him. It is time to be prophetic about the Christ we know is present in the folks who are pushed aside, dismissed, left out, undermined, underfed, unhoused, or simply unseen and unheard. It is time to hear the truth in the words of the poet Gerard Manley Hopkins:

> *For Christ plays in ten thousand places,*
> *Lovely in limbs, lovely in eyes not his,*
> *through the features of [our] faces.*

It is time for the people of God to stop marching along with the status quo in search of security, power, and control, but to stumble instead towards the margins where we will encounter a magic and a mystery that will plunge us trembling but rejoicing into the Realm of God. This is what this book is all about. And it invites all of us into such a time and such a place where we will recognize the face of Christ—always new, always unexpected. Always reminding us of God's promise:

> *I will pour out my Spirit on all humanity;*
> *your sons and daughters shall prophesy,*
> *your old ones shall dream dreams,*
> *and your young shall see visions.*
> *On all men and women*
> *will I pour out my Spirit in those days.*
> —Joel 2:28-29

In such a time indeed, and only in such a time, along with all God's prophets, fools, artists, mystics, poets, and children will we realize a new Jerusalem. The invitation is always there. God is always waiting. It is never too late to see, and to become, "Christ in the Margins."

—Edwina Gateley

FOUNDERS

The body is a unit, though it is made up of many parts . . . If one part suffers, every part suffers with it; if one part is honored, every part rejoices with it. Now you are the body of Christ, and each one of you is a part of it.

—1 CORINTHIANS 12:12, 26

The Christ of Maryknoll

I have named this icon "Christ of Maryknoll" because Maryknoll and Orbis Books mean so much to me. Both endeavor to see the Christ among the least of us, and to serve the Christ who lives in the margins of this world.

Maryknoll missioners—priests, sisters, brothers, and laity—number 1,300 strong, and endeavor to see the face of Christ and to be the face of Christ, especially among the poor, on four continents. Maryknollers are known for their commitment to Jesus' Gospel that "whatever you do to the least of these, you do unto me." They have been faithful to this vision since their founding in 1911 by James Walsh, Thomas Price, and Mary Josephine Rogers.

Today Maryknollers work in faith communities in forty countries, with people of all faiths and none, in bustling parishes with families and in war zones with refugees; they minister to orphans, the elderly, the sick, the imprisoned, and people with AIDS. Maryknollers have been imprisoned in China and elsewhere for their work among the poor, the broken, the oppressed: Orbis has taken great risks to extend the Maryknoll vision. I hope this icon will bring inspiration to all those who share in this vision.

The icon does not make clear which side of the fence Christ is on. Is he imprisoned or are we? Through our cultural institutions and personal lives we all place barriers between ourselves and true happiness. We and our institutions also try to imprison Christ in various ways, to tame him and the dangerous memories he would bring us of our goals and ideals. The Christ of Maryknoll cannot be tamed.

Christ of the Desert

Another, and older, rich Christian tradition flows out of the deserts of the Middle East. While it may seem marginal next to the Greek and Latin traditions, it is their equal in dignity and theological importance. It belongs to those churches that use Syriac as their liturgical language. Syriac is a dialect of Aramaic, the language spoken by Christ himself.

This icon celebrates the richness of Syriac Christianity. The inscriptions in the upper corners translate as "Jesus Christ," and at the bottom, "Christ of the Desert." The Syriac language has ties to the earth that are deep and fertile. It is more inclusive than most European languages. The theological experience of Syriac Christians is different because they have encountered the Gospel in this language. Theirs is an unhellenized expression—one that is neither Europeanized nor Westernized.

Semitic as it is, the Syriac tradition knows no dichotomy between the mind and heart. The heart is the center of the human person—center of intellect as well as feelings. The body and all of creation longs to be reunited with God.

A constant theme in Syriac literature is homesickness for Paradise, a desire to restore Paradise on earth. Christians pray facing east because Paradise was in the east. This longing was expressed in monastic terms in ancient times, but its implications today reach far beyond monastery walls. With earthy roots, this longing for Paradise involves concrete responses in the realms of politics, ecology, and economics. It is a longing that springs from the Christ who lives in the margins.

ST. FRANCIS OF ASSISI

Saint Francis of Assisi
(1182-1226)

Francis was a universal presence whose love extended across barriers of class, religion, and race. His reverence for everything led him to call animals, plants, and all of creation "brother" and "sister." Animals responded to his respect and love with an amazing docility. As Francis walked across medieval Europe, people caught glimpses of what Eden must have been like.

Saint Francis helped reform the Roman Catholic Church in the thirteenth century through his example of personal poverty. He simply lived the Gospel as he took monastic life into the streets. Living among the poor, his example was so compelling that soon he had thousands of followers.

Francis's great goal was to follow Jesus as closely as possible. Near the end of his life he spent forty days in solitary prayer on Mt. Alverna. During this time he asked Jesus that he might experience, as much as he could, the love, pain, and grief that Jesus had experienced in his passion. In response to his prayer he was given the stigmata—wounds in his hands, feet, and side. The wounds remained, never healing, for the rest of his life.

Before Francis died, he asked his brothers to strip him of his ragged robe so that in total poverty he might lie naked on the bare ground. He had lived on the margins as God's troubadour, a bright flame by which others could read the Gospel with fresh insight and vision.

 STE. MARGUERITE D'YOUVILLE

Saint Marguerite d'Youville
(1701-1771)

Marie Marguerite Dufrost de Lajemmerais was born at Varennes, Quebec, on October 15, 1701. Marguerite was no stranger to suffering, starting with the death of her beloved father when she was only seven. More suffering came her way when her husband, Francois d'Youville, turned out to be a gambler and bootlegger. Four of Marguerite's six children died in infancy and at the age of twenty-eight she became burdened with her husband's debts. She saw to the education of her two sons who became priests.

A deep and abiding faith in Divine Providence marked her life as she devoted all of her time and energy to caring not only for her family but for the poor and destitute who lived on the margins in Montreal. In 1737 she founded the Congregation of the Sisters of Charity, known as the "Grey Nuns." Her vision continues today through the many works of charity carried on throughout the world by the members of the six Grey Nun congregations and through the many laywomen and laymen who work in organizations founded by the Sisters of Charity.

Pope John XXIII named her the Mother of Universal Charity and she was canonized in 1990, the first Canadian-born saint. This icon of Saint Marguerite d'Youville was commissioned by the Sisters of Charity Health System in Lewiston, Maine, for its nursing facility, St. Marguerite d'Youville Pavilion.

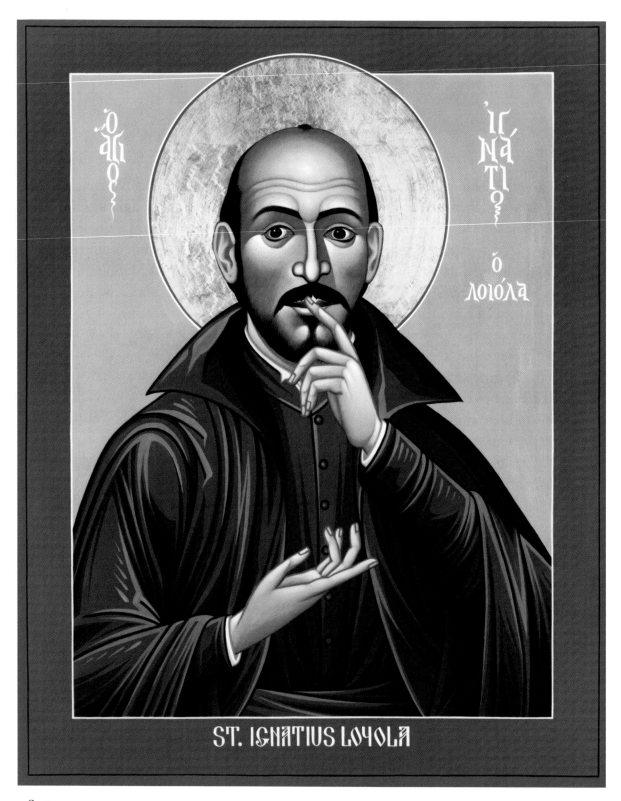

Ὁ ἅγιος Ἰγνάτιος ὁ Λοιόλα

ST. IGNATIUS LOYOLA

Saint Ignatius Loyola
(1491-1556)

Ignatius Loyola was the son of a Basque nobleman. He spent his early adult years as a soldier, until he was seriously wounded in a battle with the French. Forced to confront himself during his lengthy recovery, he ended his military career and embraced the poverty of a pilgrim. After a trip to Jerusalem, he returned to Europe and began academic studies.

His experiences during his conversion and afterwards convinced him that human beings were meant to have a direct encounter with God. Many people came to him for spiritual direction even before he was ordained a priest. After reflecting on his own experiences, he developed what he called the Exercises, as an aid for others to encounter God directly and discern God's will in their lives. In fact, his first seven followers gathered around him as a result of going through the Spiritual Exercises with him.

He and his followers felt at first that they were called to work as missionaries in Palestine. When this proved impossible, they placed themselves at the service of the pope. Called the Society of Jesus, they eventually became one of the most influential Catholic religious orders. Ignatius intended them to follow the poor and humble Jesus, serving without power, on the fringes of society and the church.

In this icon, Ignatius is inviting us to enter silently into God's presence, to encounter God within our hearts. He reminds us of our constant need to discern the spirit of our times and God's will in our lives.

ΗΓΙΑ ΚΛΆΡΑ

ST. CLARE OF ASSISI

Saint Clare of Assisi
(c. 1194-1253)

When she was eighteen years old, Clare left behind the wealth and ease of her noble family and embraced the radical poverty of Jesus, which she had heard Saint Francis praise in the streets of Assisi. For her remaining forty-one years she struggled against incredible odds to be true to her ideals. When church authorities ordered her to relax the austerity of her way of life, she patiently insisted that women could follow the Gospel ideals as well as men. Two days before her death, she finally received papal approval for the rule that she had written for her followers.

Like other women religious of her day, Clare and her companions lived within a strict monastic enclosure. What made them different was their rigorous vow of poverty, which forbade even communal possessions. They supported themselves by the work of their hands and depended on alms for the rest. They wore the simplest clothing and fasted every day except for Christmas and Sundays. In all things they strove to maintain among themselves "the unity of mutual love and peace."

For twenty-eight years Clare was continually ill, and often confined to her bed. Even in bed she insisted on doing her share of work. One legend tells of how she dropped a roll of linen cloth she was sewing, and how it rolled too far from her bed for her to reach. The monastery cat, with which she is pictured in this icon, retrieved the cloth for her so that she could finish the work. This story reflects the profound closeness to creation and all other creatures that lies at the core of Franciscan spirituality.

For forty-one years Clare led her austere life with the same small group of women, only leaving her tiny monastery once. In spite of her illness and other problems, in spite of the sorrow she must have felt as she watched many of Francis's male followers abandon his ideals after his death, her writings sparkle with peace and joy. She challenges us to re-examine our own goals, which often bring us stress and misery, as she speaks of moving us through life "with swift pace, light step, and unswerving feet, so that even your steps stir up no dust."

REFLECTION *by Edwina Gateley*

In times of relative conformity and acceptance of the status quo, they slip into human history demonstrating the amazing potential of the human spirit and leaving our communal story forever changed. They are the founders—those birthers of new ways whose courage and spirit take all of us a little bit further than we ever thought we could go. Because of them we see further and deeper, and we dare to go along paths we never imagined. They open up hitherto unknown spaces, expanding the human spirit and enriching all of us.

What is it that grasps and impels these men and woman to push beyond conventional boundaries and so delight us, ultimately, with new creative spaces? Wisdom—God's Playmate, the Feminine Principle of the Godhead—is at work, ever delighting in birthing new possibilities and inviting open hearts to rise up and respond to visions and dreams by enfleshing them. Forging new paths is no easy task. For the most part, we do not easily take to new ways and ideas—we settle into the comfort of the way things are and tend to plod along with that which makes us feel comfortable and secure. Basically, we conform.

Founders do not conform. They burst upon our flat horizon with creative alternatives and new models of being human. Not for them the mediocre, not for them the binding of the human spirit to societal, political, or religious norms. The founders, impelled by a fire within them, must create new ways for ordinary humans to become as gods. Aware of the Christ of Maryknoll who breathes in each of us, they leave the familiar to be among God's children everywhere. Inspired by Christ of the Desert, and invited to plant seeds in wilderness places, they glimpse in their struggles the Realm of God which has no bounds for our possibilities.

Because of their amazing courage in the face of hostilities and conventional narrow-mindedness, the founders make an indelible mark on human history—frequently not recognized until many years after their deaths. Initially they are often a scandal as they push against our traditional belief systems and ways of being. Ironically, but almost universally, such bright lights in our gray spaces are just as often discredited and rejected. It is as if our small hearts cannot tolerate the depth and breadth of their imagination and the vigor of their visions. We seem to desire to be blinded rather than enlightened. Ultimately we attempt to eclipse the light of our founders—pruning radical discipleship to pietistic conformity and discarding and dimming visions that took us, for a moment, to the stars. But, alas, beyond our comfort zones. In spite of our reluctance to embrace new visions, the founders create in us a stirring of fascination as we witness in their pursuits a courage beyond the norm. Do they, perhaps, remind us of our own dreams and visions abandoned as we adjust to the gray reality of our world? Do they, perhaps, bring to mind the radical words of the poet William Wordsworth who dared insinuate our divine origin in his poem "Intimations of Immortality":

> *Whither is fled the visionary gleam?*
> *Where is it now, the glory and the dream?*
> *Our birth is but a sleep and a forgetting:*
> *The soul that rises with us, our life's Star,*
> *Hath had elsewhere its setting,*
> *And cometh from afar:*
> *Not in entire forgetfulness*
> *And not in utter nakedness,*
> *But trailing clouds of glory do we come*
> *From God, who is our home.*

The founders are those who have not let go of those "trailing clouds of glory"—the embryonic divine potential that resides within each of us but is rarely tapped. Francis, Clare, Marguerite, and Ignatius became aware of being trapped in systems which did not—could not—feed the God-seed within them. The systems in which they lived and their historical circumstances were too restricted and repressive for the visions that stirred in their souls. That seed had to burst open and reach out to their sisters and brothers—specifically the poor, the anawim of the Gospel.

Founders—birthers of new ways—cannot dismiss or resist the certainty and the urgency of their call. Because of the impelling fire of that call, nothing—not convention, not power, not secular or religious authority—can prevent them from responding. No amount of patriarchal tradition or authority could take from our founders the innate presence and power of the maternal and compassionate face of God. It is such inner authority and vision that leaves us standing in awed and often reluctant admiration of these individuals who run with the Spirit.

But the work of the Spirit is not limited to founders only. We can all, one way or another, run with the Spirit. Although our traditional founders of religious communities made lasting impacts on our religious history by following their visions, such invitations, to differing degrees, are available to all of us. The Holy Spirit is not selective or exclusive—she awaits all open hearts. And this is the key: we must be courageous and radical enough to open our hearts to the new and unexpected in our own place and time. We must, through the power of the Holy Spirit, enflesh our own daring dreams and visions as we hunger for healing and beauty and fulfillment—as we strain for "clouds of glory." We must not be afraid to be founders, enfleshers of new things.

One such dream I had was to break down the barriers that we have allowed ourselves to erect between our societal classes—specifically between middle-class women and women involved in prostitution and drugs. It seems to me that as long as we separate and stay apart from one another's reality, we will not understand or enter the process of deep healing. As long as we are divided, we are diminished. And so I began to organize retreats for women recovering from prostitution and drugs in places of hospitality run by women who, for the most part, had never been exposed to such people before. For almost all of my ladies from the streets it was a first—their first vacation, their first air or train trip, their first stay in the country, and, most definitely, their first stay in a monastery! And, along with that, exposure to women from a very different life experience. One by one, walls fell as sister met sister. Together we all sat to share food and conversation—white women, black women, religious women, women from prostitution, broken women, healed women—all met and embraced and became, simply, women together. The space where it happened felt sacred and holy, and all of us suddenly felt more whole and alive.

We did things never ever done before by these ladies of the streets. We went on nature walks to collect berries and flowers and nuts; we fed and stroked llamas; we planted organic squash; we baked bread together and ate it together. We danced beneath a full moon. We told our stories and we wept together for each sister. In those days we worked miracles. There healing happened. New life emerged. Whoever would have thought that we could dance together? Whoever would have thought that there, in that little space of green fields where cows grazed and birds sang, women from such violence could be held and nurtured and loved by women so different whom they had never met before? Who would ever have thought that we could have touched such depths of glory? But we did. And none of us—ever—will be the same. It is the spirit of the founders, the spirit of wisdom and truth ever seeking wholeness and beauty, that leads us to accomplish such things.

My experience with these retreats convinces me that somehow, in some deep universal way, the same spirit that moved our founders nudges us all along into a more compassionate place in the world, that all of us are intrinsically and subconsciously connected, and that when there is healing and hope for one of us there is healing and hope for all. The seed of new beginnings, which moved within the founders of Maryknoll—James Walsh, Thomas Price, and Mary Josephine Rogers—moves within our human community today. It is our choice to listen deeply and to be open to that invitation to new life, which is never withdrawn but whispers forever within each of us:

Wisdom is bright, and does not grow dim.
By those who love her she is readily seen,
and found by those who look for her.
Quick to anticipate those who desire her,
    she makes herself known to them.
Watch for her early and you will have no trouble;
you will find her sitting at your gates.
Even to think about her is understanding fully
        grown;
be on the alert for her and anxiety will quickly
        leave you.
She walks about looking for those who are worthy of
        her
and graciously shows herself to them as they go,
in every thought of theirs coming to meet them.
                    —WISDOM 6:12–16

The founders are, indeed, worthy of the Spirit whom they have found sitting at their gates. Because of their courageous response to that Spirit, we ourselves have seen a little further and, like it or not, we will never be the same.

We have been driven by inspired and brave spirits to an awareness of new possibilities and new ways. Though we may flee because we are afraid of being stretched beyond the limits we have set for ourselves or others, deep in our psyches, the founders leave us a glimpse of "clouds of glory." And hidden in our collective story, that experience and that vision are not forgotten. Our invitation to say yes to the Spirit and to enflesh new and daring dreams will always be with us.

> Brave, reckless souls,
> these founders,
> who dare birth dreams
> and run with them
> down our city streets,
> driven by a passion
> that leaves us gasping
> in wonderment—
> and disapproval.
> Brave, reckless souls,
> these founders,
> who would change the world
> with their visions of God
> and have us
> (pouting saints and reluctant angels)
> do the same.
> Brave, reckless souls,
> these founders,
> whose lights
> we flee,
> refusing to dance
> to an unknown tune
> lest it whirl us,
> dizzying,
> into God.
> Brave, reckless souls,
> these founders,
> who in league with Wisdom
> (God's wild, free Spirit)
> forever run amongst us,
> singing aloud
> their songs of love
> and trailing
> clouds of glory!

CRUSADERS AND PROPHETS

This is my commandment:

love one another;

as I have loved you.

No one has greater love than this,

to lay down one's life for one's friends.

—JOHN 15:12-13

Bik'egu'inda'n

The Apache Christ

No people in North American history have suffered as much from stereotypes as have the Apaches. A proud, monotheistic people of the desert and mountains, their history is strikingly similar to that of the ancient Jews. The Apaches were also enslaved, to produce wealth for Spain and Mexico. The United States army carried many of them off to the swamps of Florida and Alabama as prisoners of war. Their crime had been defending their land—a land they considered holy—from invaders who respected neither their culture nor their faith. They live today on reservations hidden away in what is left to them of their sacred mountains.

This icon celebrates the beauty of Apache culture, specifically the culture of the Mescalero Apaches of New Mexico. Christ is depicted as a Mescalero holy man, greeting the sun on the fourth morning of the woman's puberty rites. These are the most sacred of the Apache ceremonies, celebrating the sanctity of the gift of producing new life. A sun symbol is painted on his left palm, and he holds a deer hoof rattle in his right hand. A basket at his feet holds an eagle feather, a grass brush, and bags of tobacco and cattail pollen—items used in the rites. He stands atop 12,000-foot Sierra Blanca, the sacred mountain of the Mescaleros. Behind him flies an eagle, the guide who first led the Apaches to their "promised land." The inscription at the bottom of the icon is Apache for "Giver of Life," one of their names for God. The letters in Christ's halo are the Greek version of that name. The Greek letters in the upper corners of the icon are abbreviations for "Jesus Christ."

Christians find truth in what they call the Old Testament. They call the ancient Jews who fought slavery and defended their land religious heroes and prophets. When the Apaches did the same thing during the last four centuries, however, Christians called them bloodthirsty savages and did their best to destroy them as a race. The Apaches have somehow survived four centuries of Christian genocide and continue to tell the stories of their heroes and prophets. Can modern Christians go beyond inherited stereotypes and find the sacred where they do not expect it? Apache prophets have much to say for those with ears to hear.

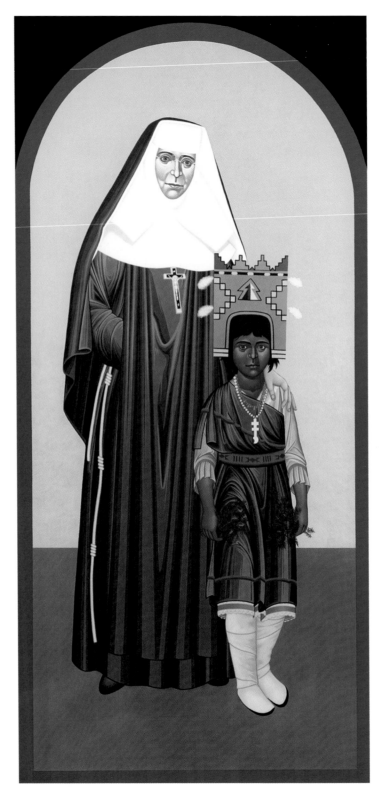

Saint Katharine Drexel
(1858-1955)

Katharine Drexel was born into a wealthy Philadelphia family. As a young woman she became aware of the suffering of Native Americans on the newly established reservations in the western part of the United States. She began using money from her inheritance to establish schools on the reservations and to send food and clothing to the people. In time she expanded her efforts to include impoverished African Americans in the southern and eastern states.

From the time she was twenty-one years old, Katharine had wanted to become a religious sister. Six years later the bishop of Omaha, Nebraska, encouraged her to found a religious community to work among Native Americans and African Americans. She founded the Sisters of the Blessed Sacrament and took vows as the first member in 1891. For forty-four years she guided her new order, founding schools in New Mexico and Arizona, and throughout the eastern half of the country. In 1917 she founded what became Xavier University in New Orleans.

In 1935 Katharine suffered a severe heart attack, and spent the remaining twenty years of her life in retirement and prayer. In this icon she stands beside a girl from San Ildefonso Pueblo in northern New Mexico. The girl is dressed for the traditional summer corn dance.

In 2001 Pope John Paul II canonized Katharine Drexel as a saint.

STEVEN BIKO of SOUTH AFRICA

Steven Biko of South Africa
(1946-1977)

Steven Biko is a martyr of South Africa. His life was spent instilling pride and a sense of identity in fellow Blacks, forced to live in the margins by the apartheid policy of the white government. Not since Hitler's Nuremberg laws has any community suffered under so monstrous a burden of racial regulations.

The quotation on the scroll he holds in the icon is how he defined "Black Power" during a court trial in 1976. The Greek inscription by his head reads "Holy Steven."

Biko was imprisoned several times for his work and was "banned." He died in prison on September 12, 1977, after being tortured and beaten. He was not a regular churchgoer, but he laid down his life for Christ. All human beings bear God's image. Whenever human dignity is abused, God's image is violated. At the Last Judgment Christ has told us he will say, "Whatsoever you did to the least of my brothers and sisters, you did to me" (Matthew 25:40).

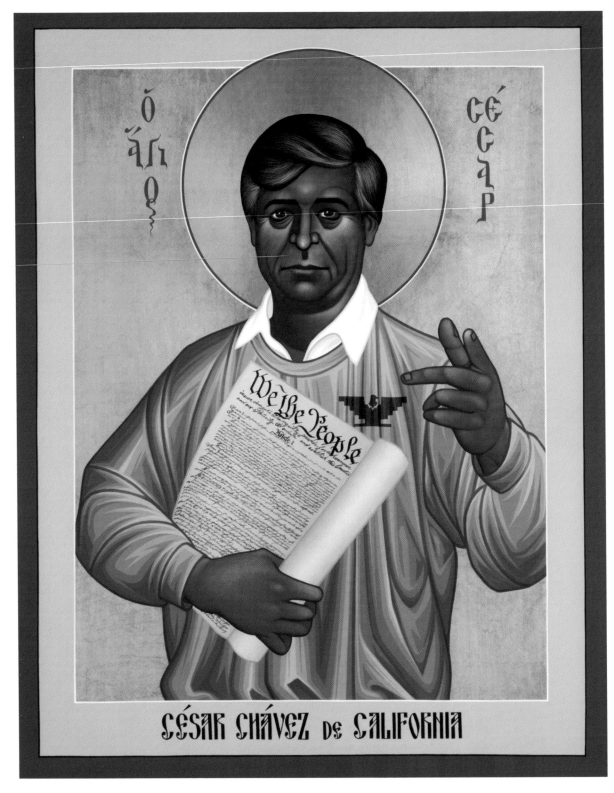

ὁ ἅγιος

ΟέCΑΡ

We the People

CÉSAR CHÁVEZ DE CALIFORNIA

César Chávez
(1927-1993)

César Chávez, champion of the poor, saw his family's home and small farm seized by creditors when he was only ten. He spent his youth as a migrant worker, traveling with his family wherever there were crops to harvest. They shared what little they had with those who had less.

Work in the fields meant long hours of backbreaking tasks and exposure to dangerous pesticides for half the wages other workers in the United States could expect. Migrant workers had no rights and lived at the mercy of employers. This experience of helplessness and poverty engendered in César a profound thirst for justice. From 1952 until his death, he worked ceaselessly to improve the lot of his people.

After ten years of working in voter registration drives and in challenging police and immigration abuse, he turned his attention to the struggle for justice for migrant workers. Using nonviolent tactics and sustained by the deep spirituality of his Catholic Mexican roots, he led the United Farm Workers through seemingly impossible situations. Agribusiness sometimes responded with violence. Several union members were killed. Even the Teamsters tried to sabotage what gains his union made. In spite of all odds, he made the plight of migrants known to the rest of the nation, giving a voice to those who had been forgotten.

Always a poor man, César sometimes had to ask for food for his wife and children from the very workers he was trying to organize. He died on April 22, away from home on union business, after an eight-day water-only fast. An estimated thirty-five thousand people formed his three-mile-long funeral procession. He was buried as a poor man in a simple pine box. He remains in our midst, however, as a patron of all the poor, but especially of immigrant minorities who suffer solely because they will not watch their families starve. In this icon he carries the Constitution of the United States, for whose guarantees he fought on behalf of all the oppressed.

THESE THINGS WERE NOT DONE BY SAVAGES AND PAGANS, THEY WERE DONE BY THE CHRISTIAN CHURCH!

ELIZABETH CADY STANTON

Elizabeth Cady Stanton
(1815-1902)

As we begin the twenty-first century, there are few who would argue that European culture, now scattered across so much of the globe, is going through a major upheaval. In fact, it has been several millennia since this culture has been challenged and shaken so deeply. The fall of Rome and the rise of Christianity, the age of discovery, even the industrial revolution all pale in comparison with what began in the mid-nineteenth century when Elizabeth Cady Stanton and a few other courageous women dared to question the marginalized status of women in the Judaeo-Christian world.

Elizabeth might have looked forward to a life of structured leisure, coming as she did from an old, monied, Protestant family on the east coast. In spite of her privileged position, however, she was denied a formal higher education simply because she was a woman. This opened her eyes to the marginalized status of all women in her world, both rich and poor alike, and propelled her into a life of tireless crusading for social change.

In July of 1848, in Seneca Falls, New York, she led a group of women to call the world's first convention to discuss women's rights. The resulting *Declaration of Sentiments* dared to criticize both Church and State for the many ways each held women in a subordinate position. For the next half century Elizabeth's voice rose loud and clear against the many injustices against women that Christian culture had perpetrated for so many centuries. In 1895 she published a commentary on the Bible in which she criticized and expanded on texts she deemed demeaning to women.

Although she worked most of her life with her close friend Susan B. Anthony, after her death the women's movement marginalized her memory and exalted Anthony in her place. Elizabeth had been too controversial and outspoken, especially against Christian institutions. Most women wanted to put forward a more respectable face for their movement. It is only in our day that Elizabeth is once again recognized for her rightful place in history. While some continue to curse the upheaval she began, and many long for what they imagine to be "the good old days" when everyone knew their place, history will ultimately recall the beginning of Elizabeth Cady Stanton's crusade as the moment when European culture was given a new lease on life.

REFLECTION *by Edwina Gateley*

Given certain conditions and challenges, the human spirit is capable of astounding achievements. It is evident from our history that we can stretch ourselves into spaces that, under normal circumstances, would leave us trembling and utterly incapable of any action. And there are those amongst us—brave and indignant souls—who, at a certain point, in the face of oppression, injustice, cruelty, or inhumanity, can no longer hold back and remain silent and unresponsive. It is as if a saturation point is reached at which there arises within them a resounding or, indeed, a passionately whispered no that impels them to radical and prophetic action. They are the crusaders and the prophets, those who dare to stand over and against an unacceptable reality no matter what the danger or the consequences. Their courage, integrity, and the fire of their convictions leave most of us standing open-mouthed in awe and admiration. What perhaps leaves us in such a state of astonishment is the deep awareness that such giants as Steven Biko, César Chávez, and Elizabeth Cady Stanton, like most crusaders and prophets, were rather ordinary folks in the first place. They became extraordinary when they aligned themselves with justice in a very real and life-changing way—when they reached a point where they refused to settle for less than human dignity and did it to such a degree that their lives were put on the line.

Crusaders and prophets are like that. Something they believe in is so deep and passionate that it becomes bigger than anything else—even bigger than their own need for safety and well-being. They become capable, in those amazing moments, or years of grace, of rising beyond their fears and inadequacies and touching extraordinary heights of courage. They expand the human spirit to the edges of divine courage. And, in doing so, give all of us a glimpse of our possibilities.

The crusaders and prophets remind us of the Christ who openly witnessed to the intrinsic divine presence within humanity and dared tell all who listened to him that they were precious in God's eyes. The radical implication of such a message is that it recognizes and names the equality and dignity of all humanity—including the very poor, the different, and those who speak with a critical voice. This claim to equality and dignity is a threat to all forms of power, hierarchy, and status. One must unleash within oneself a powerful and prophetic spirit that dares to speak against the principalities and powers that rule over the anawim, the little ones of our world so beloved by Christ. Yet that spirit—powerful and simple—continues to be unleashed today and creates prophetic figures in our human story. It becomes more than a message. It becomes a mission. It shines in the eyes of the Apache Christ—challenging us to go beyond our boundaries.

When oppression and violence threaten or destroy human dignity, those who hold all human beings precious in God's eyes and are vulnerable to the spiritual power within them cannot stand by. They must follow the path of Jesus and other great prophets and crusaders who have gone before them. They must, and they do, dare to speak, dare to march, and dare even to die for their beliefs, because all of us—whatever our race, religion, sexual orientation, gender, or background—all of us are made in the image and likeness of God.

We forget that. Getting so many knocks and bruises in the course of our lives, and suffering so many set-backs and failures, we often feel helpless and insignificant and forget that we are precious in God's eyes. Over time, constantly exposed to escalating violence and injustice in our world, we tend to forget the powerful witness of Jesus and the centrality of human dignity that is affirmed by all the world's major religious traditions. But much more widespread and insidious is our habit of constantly *diluting* our responsibility to honor and preserve human dignity in the mistaken belief that there's not much we can do about it anyway. We are duped by oppressive forces in our society into feeling helpless. Somewhere along the line (though with a little discomfort and guilt), we tend to quietly leave behind our sisters and brothers to focus, instead, on our own survival and well-being. We forget we are called to be as gods.

It is not surprising that we lean towards ourselves and those in our immediate family. It is extremely difficult to break out of the security boundaries we set around ourselves. Overwhelmed by the world's excesses and atrocities, one after the other, our sensitivities are bombarded day after day with media messages of war, violence, terrorism, and escalating poverty. What are we to do? Our trembling hearts dive for cover and we do everything possible to insulate ourselves from the exposure to pain. Ironically, within such a context of apathy and despair, the prophetic spirit arises. For all our defenses there is an eternal vulnerability about the human spirit that is capable of breaking through the most fearful and resistant souls.

We are not born prophetic and courageous. We become prophetic and courageous. We have all heard stories of ordinary people suddenly and amazingly standing up for what they believe is right or marching in protest against what they believe is wrong. Testimony to such a spirit was reflected in a news report about hundreds of Russian mothers protesting the Russian army's invasion of Chechnya in 1995. According to this report grieving and desperate Russian mothers descended on the war-torn city of Grozny to find their sons and to persuade them to desert the army. The report continues:

The mothers, wearing black combat boots and carrying small Russian icons of Jesus for protection, are stopping at nothing to find their sons:

•They've locked arms and stopped a column of Russian tanks leaving the militia base at nearby Mosdak until Russian commanders let them in.

•They've entered Grozny's war-torn presi–dential palace, the target of massive Rus–sian bombing Thursday, to gather the names of Russian soldiers being held in the basement by Chechen rebels.

•They've walked among Grozny's sniper-ridden streets hoping to identify the dozens of dead, rotting Russian soldiers.

Up to 60 Russian soldiers have left with their mothers to return to Moscow, where they are now in hiding.

At least a dozen other moms and their sons, who can't afford the $49 plane and train fare back to Moscow, reportedly are hiding with ethnic Russians in this bombed-out city.

Sympathetic military commanders are allowing the soldiers to leave if their mothers come after them.

"We'd never forgive ourselves if these women were killed here," said a Russian Army Captain.

"It's a mother's duty to be here," said Elena Overchenka, of Murmansk, yelling for her son in a glass-strewn alley.

As she spoke, two Russian helicopters began blasting the palace 200 yards away.

"We won't let our government sacrifice our boys," she said kneeling down and covering her ears. "This is stupid."

Chechen rebels are often protecting the Russian mothers and offering them hot tea and bread and shelter with local families.

(*USA Today*, JANUARY 1995)

No doubt about it, those middle-aged, boot-clad, icon-armed mothers were essentially no different from any other mothers around the globe. But, at a certain point, they said "enough" to the senseless killing and brutality. Their hearts longed for peace and longed to save their boys. They crossed over the line of safety and risked their lives because they were driven by something more important than themselves—the value of human dignity and the preciousness of human life. During the 1994-96 war around 3,500 soldiers were brought home by their mothers (*Guardian Weekly*, October 1999). The message became a mission; it made these nondescript Russian women into crusaders.

They do not stand alone. All over the globe women and men are standing up against vio-lence and risking their lives with prophetic ges-tures of protest. Another report in the mid 1990s tells of a Turkish widow whose husband was killed in a fight with Kurdish rebels. The young woman refused to play the traditional part of the courageous officer's widow, declaring:

"My husband did his duty but he did not believe the problem in the south-east would be solved by killing or being killed. I don't see him as a martyr. He is a victim of dirty politics."

Her attitude has shocked many Turks, especially in the armed forces. But the officer's widow did not stop there. On September 2 she appeared in public holding hands with the sister of a PKK activist who had also been killed. Together they made an appeal to stop the killing.

(*Guardian Weekly*, SEPTEMBER 1995)

The public protest against war made by this young widow brought her into direct conflict with conservative politicians and journalists as well as the Turkish army. Her message of conciliation made her a modern crusader.

The story is also told of how a group of women gathered together in a cemetery in Tuzla, the former Yugoslavia, and decorated the cemetery with symbols of doves, crosses, and crescents—symbols of their different religions in a country rife with ethnic and religious hatred and intolerance. The women were, in fact, burying their slaughtered children together in the same grave. When questioned by journalists observing this extraordinary event, the women replied that they were doing it for "the future." They had a dream, and in the midst of all the division, the violence, and the hatred these prophetic women declared it.

A similar event took place in Rwanda at the height of the genocide of the Tutsi people by the majority Hutu. As both Tutsi and Hutu were killed and killing, a Tutsi woman sheltered orphans from both tribes, thereby risking death herself from either side.

Unprecedented violence today is unleashing unprecedented prophetic acts of compassion and healing. As more and more individuals reach the saturation point where they can no longer tolerate what they know, deep down, is inhuman, change will come about. For every Biko, for every Chávez, for every marching or protesting mother, there are thousands of others not yet marching, not yet speaking, but listening and wondering deep in their souls. Every prophet and every crusader who stands for human dignity and freedom stands for all

of us. And someday we will see, and begin to understand, and we ourselves will begin to change because of the prophetic witness we have seen and the truth that we know in our hearts. That is an essential aspect of prophecy. It shifts us to a different place—no matter how long it might take—where human consciousness is ultimately affected and slowly changed. Our contemporary world, suffering from so much hunger, poverty, war, and fear is desperately in need of such a change. We have to make a difference.

One way or another every one of us is called to be something of a crusader and a prophet. For if we are faithful to our call to be a Gospel People, we cannot but be aware that, in these troubled times, we are far from the Realm of God on earth. Vast numbers of our sisters and brothers in the developing world live with disease, poverty, and famine. Infectious diseases, AIDS, TB, and malaria (which we in the Northern Hemisphere have the resources and the skills to alleviate or cure) are responsible for half of all deaths in the developing world. In Africa AIDS has left 13 million children orphaned. The drugs that suppress the AIDS virus and keep people well in the North are too expensive for most of the poor world's 40 million infected. Out of 1,393 new medicines brought to the market between 1975 and 1999 only 16 were for tropical diseases and TB (*Guardian Weekly*, August 2002). The reality is that profit, not need, drives the development of new medicines. Such an unjust system calls for—demands—the prophetic voice, the voice of the Gospel. We cannot turn a blind eye to the Christ who suffers from AIDS, TB, and malaria. And we cannot be silent before the fact that we in the rich world have the resources, though not yet the will, to change that reality.

Throughout the world 125 million children are not attending school because of poverty. The cost of providing universal primary education is close to $86 billion a year—the equivalent of four days of military spending around the world. Clearly, our priorities are askew. Clearly, our collective prophetic voice needs to rise loudly enough to be heard in our congressional corridors, our houses of power, and our corporate boardrooms throughout our affluent Northern Hemisphere.

According to a United Nations Report (2002), at the current rate of progress it will be 130 years before the world is free from hunger. We who follow the Christ know that we must feed the hungry. And we know that we must do it now. We will not, must not, wait 130 years. We must be prophetic. We must speak aloud. We must march. And be crusaders.

It is said that the critical mass is 11 percent. That is all that is needed to begin to change the world and to create a shift at the grassroots level. We do not need many crusaders and prophets—only that sacred 11 percent. As we bestir ourselves to make a difference in our world we can take comfort in the fact that we do not have to be brave or prophetic for a *long* time. Most of our lives can, hopefully, be lived out plodding happily and peacefully along. But there will always come times—perhaps only moments—when, impelled by a stirring of grace in our bellies, we cry out loud or take to the streets in the name of justice. Then, joining the ranks of Biko, Chávez, Katharine Drexel, and Elizabeth

Cady Stanton, we will truly demonstrate how precious we are in God's eyes—and our eyes. We will stand up, we will march, we will speak, and we will be prophets and crusaders. For that prophetic moment, we will be given all the grace and courage we will need. And the world will never be the same.

Crusaders and prophets,
brave souls,
bursting with indignation
against violence
wrought upon their
brothers and sisters,
daring to march
in boots and sandals
through mud and bushland
and rocky terrain,
daring to erect
podiums
on flat scorched earth,
and stand tall
amidst the broken,
calling them
to rise and march
into the jaws of hell.

Crusaders and prophets,
wild children
of a passionate God
who sets their hearts
on fire,
demanding bread
in the wilderness,
water in desert places,
and blossoms to grow
in bombed-out craters.

Crusaders and prophets,
small souls,
standing over and against

swollen giants
and steel tanks—
David before Goliath—
holding aloft
a bit of stone
to shatter
the mighty system
with a little bit of light,
a little bit of yeast,
a little bit of salt—
daring to pit a seed of faith
against cold evil.

Crusaders and prophets,
ridiculous, wondrous
icons of grace,
searing us with
the heat of their fire,
and blinding us
with their shining.

Crusaders and prophets,
standing amidst the dying
and deafening us
with their marching
as they carry the brokenhearted,
whispering words
of healing
in bloodied, dried-out places.

Crusaders and prophets,
God's grace unleashed in hell,
dancing in the darkness
demanding
the blind see
and the deaf hear
as the voice of the dumb
shatters the mountain tops.

OUTCASTS

While he was at dinner in the house it happened that a number of tax collectors and sinners came to sit at the table with Jesus and his disciples. When the Pharisees saw this, they said to his disciples, "Why does your Master eat with tax collectors and sinners?"

When he heard this he replied, "It is not the healthy who need the doctor but the sick. Go and learn the meaning of the words: What I want is mercy, not sacrifice. *And indeed I did not come to call the virtuous, but sinners."*

—MATTHEW 9:10-13

يسوع المسيح

THE GOOD SHEPHERD

Christk the Good Shepherd

How often we try to tame the dangerous memories of our tradition so that they fit into a warm and fuzzy piety that does not challenge or discomfort us. The Christ who came to turn the world upside-down and inside-out becomes a simpering bearded-lady in popular art. We support the status quo and drive prophets from our midst!

When I was asked to paint an icon of the Good Shepherd for a racially mixed inner-city parish in Connecticut, I agreed on the condition that there would be no cute wooly lambs anywhere near him. During my years in monasteries, I had sometimes worked as a shepherd and I knew from experience some of the reality behind Gospel metaphors. The Good Shepherd is about sinners, the people we push to the margins, the ones we want to forget or even destroy. He is about addicts and sex-offenders and shysters and punks. If I were going to paint the Good Shepherd, he was going to be holding a goat, and not just any goat, a smelly, lustful, scary old billy goat.

I hated taking care of the monastery billy goats. Most medieval symbolism for the devil is derived from goat physiognomy. You can smell them from quite a distance, and the expression "horny" was originally applied to them. My Christ would hug such a beast to remind puritanical America that God's ways are not to be confused with ours. Because of my deep Franciscan roots I have always tried to afford animals the same dignity in my icons I would give human and divine figures. I painted this goat hair by hair and was surprised at the end when he seemed ready to leap into my arms. There was too much of me in the goat that I did not want to acknowledge and see. He demanded that I embrace myself with compassion and look at other human beings with new understanding.

Each of our souls has billy-goat parts. These are potential treasure troves of spiritual energy that can be tamed and brought in from the margins. The Puritan fears contamination from this energy, and so he cuts himself off and starves. Christ the Good Shepherd coaxes us back to wholeness and health.

Ὅ ἅγιος ΜΑΡΤΙΝΟС

Valeriana

Salvia

SAN MARTÍN DE PORRES

Saint Martin de Porres
(1579-1639)

Martin de Porres was the unwanted child of a Spanish grandee and a freed African slave. He was born in Lima, Peru, scarcely forty years after the bloody destruction of the Inca Empire. He raised himself, for the most part, and became an apprentice to a barber-surgeon so that he would have a trade. At fifteen, he began his long relationship with the Dominican Order, first as a tertiary and then as a brother with vows.

His painful childhood taught him compassion and generosity. As a Dominican he doctored Lima's sick. While surgery was primitive in his day, he had a vast knowledge of herbal medicines. With herbs he treated illnesses ranging from infections and fevers to intestinal ailments and sprains. In addition to his free services as a doctor, he distributed enormous amounts of food and clothing to the poor each week—all of which he had first begged from wealthy families. He founded an orphanage for abandoned children and staffed it with the best teachers, nurses, and guardians he could hire. On the hills near Lima, he planted fruit orchards for the poor. He is also remembered for his love of animals.

He wore the oldest, most patched garments he could find, and spent long hours in prayer. Other Dominicans sometimes found him suspended in the air many feet above the church floor, in ecstatic prayer before the large crucifix. During his lifetime he was called the "flying brother," because of the many times he bilocated in distant places like the Philippines, Japan, or North Africa, and was seen there by Peruvian merchants who knew him. He was also gifted with prophecy and clairvoyance.

He died at the age of sixty, during a severe fever. His beloved poor never allowed his memory of life in the margins to fade, and today he is one of the most popular saints of the Americas.

المدأة
السورية
الفينيقية

THE SYRO-PHOENICIAN WOMAN

The Syro-Phoenician Woman

He left that place and set out for the territory of Tyre. There he went into a house and did not want anyone to know he was there, but he could not go unrecognized. A woman whose little daughter had an unclean spirit heard about him straightaway and came and fell at his feet. Now the woman was a pagan, by birth a Syro-Phoenician, and she begged him to cast the devil out of her daughter. And he said to her, "The children should be fed first, because it is not fair to take the children's food and throw it to the house dogs." But she spoke up, "Ah yes sir," she replied, "but the house dogs under the table can eat the children's scraps." And he said, "For saying this you may go home happy: the devil has gone out of your daughter." So she went off to her home and found the child lying on the bed and the devil gone.

—MARK 7:24-30

Ὁ ΆΓΙ Ο ΙΩ ΔΗ ΔΑ ΚΟ

ΜΡ ΘV

JUAN DIEGO OF MEXICO

Juan Diego Cuauhtlacuatzin
(1474-1548)

Ten years after the bloody Spanish conquest of Mexico, the Mother of God appeared to an Aztec craftsman named Juan Diego Cuauhtlacuatzin. She appeared as an Aztec herself and addressed him in Nahuatl, the Aztec tongue, in a manner one would address a prince. She appeared several miles outside Mexico City, which had become the center of Spanish power. She insisted that a shrine in her honor be built on that spot among the conquered people. She sent Juan Diego back to the Spanish clergy to "evangelize" them—the ones who felt they already had all the truth. In each of these ways she restored dignity and hope to native people who had been dehumanized by foreign oppression.

A shrine was later built where Mary appeared, and Cuauhtlacuatzin spent the remaining seventeen years of his life there, repeating her message of hope and liberation to all who would come. About eight million Native Americans chose to become Christians in response to this message from the margins.

In every age the miracle of Guadalupe will remind the church that those the church alienates are precisely the ones who have the gifts she needs so badly to grow and be reformed. No one is completely enlightened. We must each proclaim the Gospel—and hear it proclaimed from one another.

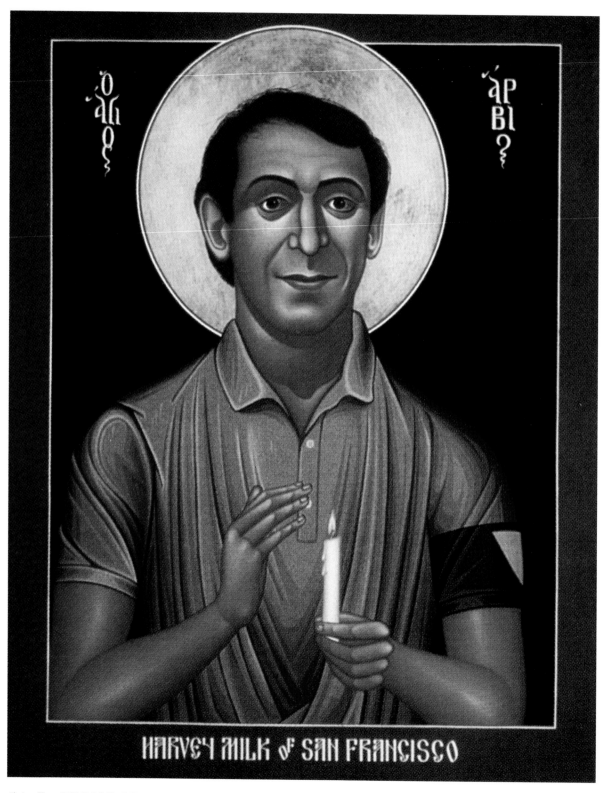

Ό ἉΓΙΟ Ἅ΄ΡΒΙΟ

HARVEY MILK of SAN FRANCISCO

Harvey Milk of San Francisco
(1930-1978)

Harvey Milk was the first openly gay person to be elected to high public office in the United States. He was not a professional politician, but ran for city supervisor in San Francisco because he felt ordinary people were being pushed to the margins by monied interests. "It takes no money to respect the individual," he said. "The people are more important than roads." As supervisor he fought consistently for the rights of all of those without a voice. These people included blue-collar workers, the elderly, racial minorities, and gay men and women.

Cardinal Juan Fresnos of Chile has said, "Whosoever stands up for human rights stands up for the rights of God." His words are an echo of what Christ has told us he will say at the Last Judgement, "Whatever you did to the least of my brothers and sisters, you did to me." Despite all the emphasis Christians put on their sexual ethics, Christ's one question at the end of time will deal with concrete acts of love and compassion.

The day of his election, Harvey tape recorded his last testament, in which he acknowledged that he would most probably die violently. The last words of that message were, "You gotta give them hope." On November 27, 1978, he was shot five times at close range by another politician who was infuriated by his defense of gay and lesbian people. That night 40,000 people, men and women, old and young, gay and straight, kept candlelight vigil outside City Hall.

In this icon he holds a candle, keeping vigil himself for the oppressed of the world. He wears a black armband with a pink triangle. This was a Nazi symbol for homosexuals, and it represents all those who have been tortured or killed because of cultural fears regarding human sexuality. Their number continues to grow with each passing year, and the compassionate Christ continues to say, "Whatever you did to the least of my brothers and sisters, you did to me."

REFLECTION *by Edwina Gateley*

The Syro-Phoenician Woman, St. Martin de Porres, Juan Diego, and Harvey Milk, all from different ages spanning the last 2000 years, have a major common denominator: they have all been identified as outcasts and, indeed, would still today be marginalized by much of modern society. One was a woman of a despised and lowly caste; one was black; one was a poor Indian peasant; and one was gay. As such they did not quite fit into what society deemed acceptable moral norms and so suffered some form of rejection—effectively they were put in their place, which was at the bottom of our hierarchical moral ladder. Such stereotyping of the people of God is firmly challenged by the surprising icon of the Good Shepherd with the billy goat. All belong to Christ.

The lens of the Gospel provides us with a deeper and more honest vision. We come to see, as we ponder on the lives and words of these so-called outcasts, a beauty and an integrity that shines fiercely on our dark horizons, challenging our veiled sight. We are startled by the icon of Christ with the billy goat—aware that this image is unconventional, not the well-loved and familiar image of Christ embracing a fluffy, cute little lamb. Such an image is indeed comforting. It feeds our need for security. On the other hand the billy goat is an affront to our dignity and serenity—it sim-

ply does not fit. Nor do the poor fit. The lepers and the broken do not fit. They are an affront to our dignity and serenity, people with AIDS, drug addicts, women in prostitution, refugees, homosexuals . . . The marginalized in our world are legion. And they threaten us. But they are embraced by the Christ with the billy goat. We are reminded of what we are to be about. This icon shifts us to another level of awareness. So will our level of consciousness shift and deepen as we dare to become more aware of and concerned for the marginalized and outcasts of our world.

We cannot but be left standing in amazement at the stark and indignant honesty of the Syro-Phoenician woman who stretched Jesus to a deeper understanding of his call to be inclusive; at the courageous witness of Harvey Milk as he put his life on the line to follow his conscience and to be true to who he was; and the breathtaking love of Martin de Porres for the poor and the despised of his time.

These "outcasts" bear a message that still desperately needs to be heard today. No amount of prayer, ritual, tithing, or good deeds will release God's grace in our hearts until and unless we come to embrace in equality all of God's people regardless of color, race, creed, or sexual orientation. We are brothers and sisters by virtue of our humanity—each one precious in God's eyes, each one a Temple of the Holy Spirit, each one God's Work of Art. The miracle and the beauty are found in our very diversity; the degree to which we embrace and cherish such diversity will be the measure of God's spirit in us. We are a tiny people called to grow in God-awareness; such spiritual growth cannot be separated from human love. In this process of becoming, God is ever at work—presenting us with an endless succession of opportunities throughout our lives to stretch our small hearts to grow, to encompass one another in love. It is a mandate which never ceases to call us to deeper wisdom, for often, when we imagine we are "liberated" and open, God will surprise us with a situation or event that reveals to us, yet again, that our hearts are not yet wide enough for the Realm of God—all of it.

Just such an event happened to me when I was living in a home for women recovering from a lifestyle of drugs and prostitution in Chicago. One night there was a knock on the door. Standing on the step with tears rolling down her face was a stunningly beautiful young woman with long blonde hair and wide blue eyes. Her name was Anna and she was a call girl who had apparently hit rock bottom and was desperate to get out of her lifestyle of prostitution. Naturally I welcomed her and, after hearing her story of abuse and violence, invited her to stay in our home and participate in our program for women in recovery.

After a few days it was clear that the other residents in our home did not like or welcome our newcomer. There were resentful looks and on-going mumbling and grumbling. "We don't like her," the women complained. "She don't fit." No amount of pleading and reasoning could placate their hostility towards Anna. After a few days observing these goings on I called Anna and sat down with her. "Anna, you haven't been honest with me, have you?" I challenged. Her face contorted as she shook her lovely head. Tears began to roll fast and free down her cheeks. "Anna," I continued, "you're a man, aren't you?" Anna sobbed and shook. "Yes . . . I'm a man," she cried, tossing back her long wavy hair. "Why didn't you tell me?" I asked. "Why didn't you tell me that you're a man?" I will never forget the look, not the response, that I was given. "If I had told you who I am," said Anna, "if I had told you that I am a man, a queen, a queer, a faggot, you would never have let me into your house, would you?"

The challenge rang loudly in the small lounge—it assailed every little, vulnerable nerve ending that my moral, righteous, Christian body contained as I spluttered: "Well . . . Well . . . no . . . you see . . . it's just that . . . we work with . . . well . . . we don't have facilities for . . . " I trailed off, then admitted to Anna and to myself: "No. If I had known, I guess I would not have let you stay." In that moment of faltering transparent protest as I struggled within the small moral box that I had built for myself, another awareness surged from some deep hidden place within me and I heard the words echoing in my soul: "My Kingdom is for all. For black and white, and gay and straight, and transgender. They are all mine. I have created them for myself. I dare you . . . I dare you to love them all."

In that moment I knew without a doubt that God in Anna was leading me, teaching me, and taking me to a deeper place of love if I would dare go there—a place of integrity in which all are loved and worthy in God's sight. Receiving, embracing, and loving Anna was integral to my own wholeness. In that moment I knew that I needed Anna more than she needed me. I knew also that my vision was a little clearer and my compassion a little deeper. Anna stayed with us. And all of us were richer for her presence.

The love I felt for Anna almost broke my heart the day I received a collect call from her in jail. She had been picked up the previous night for soliciting and had spent the rest of the night in "lock-up"—the men's lock-up. I went to bail her out. Anna was led from the cell and tears came to my eyes as I saw the cruelty wreaked on those whom society despises. Anna was visibly trembling. Her long blonde hair was disheveled and her mascara was streaked down her face. She clearly had been left to the mercy of the other men in the lock-up. She sobbed in shame and humiliation as the police sniggered and grinned behind her. Anna, over six feet tall, still wore the pink frilly dress she had been wearing when she had been arrested the night before. I agonized before her brokenness and the brutality of our incarceration system. I was grateful that I was there for Anna, and that she was there to remind me and to challenge me to set the prisoners free.

There are many in our world who are labeled outcasts but who may be, in effect, angels and messengers sent to draw us closer to God. Our task is to recognize who they are. One whom I recognized was called May. She was the manager of the local brothel to which I was invited as a guest.

On my first visit I was very nervous. Why, I pondered, did I ever agree to accept the invitation at all? No one in their right mind, I argued with myself, would ever set foot in such an establishment. They might well be legal in Nevada, but definitely not in midwest Chicago where one read from time to time of police raids on such hives of immorality. I could well end up in jail for simply being present in a house of prostitution. But, struggling with a soul instinct that this might indeed be a call from God, I had given in to the enthusiastic entreaties of one of the brothel workers who even managed to half convince me that I would be welcome by May, the brothel manager. Unable to dismiss the urgent sense of divine call in my guts, I finally found myself standing before an anonymous-looking gray building on the corner of a busy street. Who was I to argue with God? Or, for that matter, to have the remotest understanding of God's ways? I rang the doorbell.

May peered cautiously through the crack between the door and the entranceway. "Sister?" she whispered urgently, ushering me rapidly into the lobby as she closed the door behind us. Clearly and erroneously, May thought that I was a nun—I hoped it would not make a difference to my being welcomed when she learned that I was not a religious sister. We both scurried like guilty intruders up a set of steps and through another door into a darkened room filled with huge potted plants and heavy drapes.

"Take the lady's coat and hang it up," May barked at a small figure hovering nervously nearby. My coat was promptly carried off into yet deeper darkness. Two cats were gently shooed off a large floral armchair I was motioned to sit on.

The madam was like anybody's grand-mother. Small in stature, she stared up at me through thick lenses that doubled the size of her blue eyes. Her gray hair encircled her well-lined face in neatly permed curls. I guessed her age to be in the mid seventies. Preliminaries were extremely difficult. What does one say in a working brothel? Very little, it turned out. Hardly had I sat down than the phone rang and May grabbed it like a lifeline. Her voice changed. Her face changed. She was practically purring as she proceeded to describe to the (obviously male) voice on the other end of the line how many girls were available, what their vital statistics were, and how accomplished they were in sexual matters. I wished I could disappear. May's voice was honeyed and entic-ing. She should be in theater I thought. "See you soon then, darling," she breathed down the line. The phone was slammed down and May yelled towards the darkened doorway: "Customer, Lisa!"

And so the day continued. I sat and watched the endless pattern of activity—phone calls, furtive male figures hurrying past into the bedrooms beyond, water running, doors quietly closing, and, all the while, the elderly lady called May stood guard by the phone and the door, eternally vigilant. In the midst of all the activity she kept a constant brew of coffee going and a smell of home cooking wafted from what must have been the kitchen area.

"I take care of my girls," she repeatedly and proudly assured me. "I always cook them a good dinner—else they'd eat nothing, or just stuff themselves with junk. They don't get no

junk in my house." May insisted that I too have "a good dinner" when I was eventually graduated from the entrance lounge to the kitchen where "the girls" sat around the table waiting for the clients to call. In the kitchen the atmosphere was relaxed. The women smoked, joked, drank endless cups of coffee, and told "war" stories of their encounters with pimps and clients. May sat and watched them maternally, for all the world like a grandmoth-er with her granddaughters—urging them to eat more and smoke less and advising them on a myriad of questions from relationships with men to make-up, hygiene, and cooking tips.

"I'm all they have," she whispered to me when the women were working. "I bail them out of jail, and I give them a bed if they're stuck. They're safe here." Her intense blue eyes appealed to me for acceptance and approval. "It's better than the streets," she assured me defensively. Yes, I knew it was. I felt miserable at the sad reality of it all.

When Thanksgiving came around, May cooked a huge turkey and laid out a wonderful spread for her "girls"—and for me. After we had eaten May insisted that all of us take doggy bags home for our families. For the first time, and having no family in the United States, I began to realize (and not without a sense of awe) that this, indeed, was my family. I had no need of a doggy bag.

One day May pressed a $20 bill into my hand. "This is for your mission," she whispered. I was astounded. "As long as there are men," she continued, "I will never go out of business, so you are always welcome to a share."

Over the years the madam plied me with donations and gifts. Deep down I knew she was trying to buy my love and approval. But she did not need to. I came to love May. I came to see beyond her business to a houseful of women doing the only thing they believed they could do and, in the midst of their transparent pain and fear, caring for each other, looking out for each other, and desperately trying to earn enough money to pay for their rent and take care of their kids. They were well aware that their clients were respected, middle-class men from the business world and the suburbs, and they well knew that these very same men who used them also despised and abused them. But, desperate to survive in a world that did not love them or care for them, May's girls sat, week after week, month after month, waiting and hoping for a client who might tip them well. ("My daughter needs new shoes . . ." "I gotta get another $20 for groceries . . ." and so it went on.) May, ever watchful for their needs, would slip them extra dollars here and there. "And pay it back!" she would snap at the grateful recipient. Glancing over at me on one such occasion, she added: "They never do. But I don't expect them to. They have no manners. Not a clue about what's right. They think I forget." She laughed. "But I never forget." The brothel was not only a dysfunctional family—it was also a place of survival and ambiguity. Love, pain, and resentment resided here in unhappy and dismal union. The brothel broke my heart.

One evening, as a winter darkness fell around the gaudy street lamps and the traffic slowed with the oncoming night, May and I sat together around the now empty kitchen table. The last client had left. All the girls were gone. In the unaccustomed silence that left the little kitchen suddenly stilled and vulnerable, the madam looked at me. And then she crumpled weeping. As I held her frail and aged body she spoke hoarsely from a place deep within. "Thank you . . . Thank you for loving us," she sobbed. "We are so lonely. We are all so lonely."

In the darkening brothel, holding the sobbing elderly lady, we were both, oh, so lonely. And night fell upon us.

Though many would reject and condemn May for her profession, I came to love her. For all her diminishment, there shone in her a deep and beautiful humanity that I was privileged to glimpse. Who knows the soul of another and who can truly judge another? It was only as I grew close to May that I came to see behind the masks—masks that she wore in order to hide a lifetime of hurt, violence, and vulnerability. Masks that only compassion could penetrate. It was clear to me that May experienced being an outcast and knew herself as an outcast. Her self-hatred often revealed itself in moments of anger and verbal violence. It was during such moments that I knew, intuitively, of how God longed to hold and comfort her. I knew her as Beloved. It is, perhaps, hard for us to understand such a love. But one's experience of it cannot be doubted. May was loved. The tragedy was that she would never know it—could not, in fact, ever know it, simply because it was beyond her belief. But I knew it. And it has changed me. May has changed me. She was my sister. I shall never forget May. And I shall never forget Stanley.

Stanley always brought joy to my heart in the despairing streets where I used to walk. Whenever he saw me, Stanley would do a little dance of delight and his face would light up as he pranced across the street to hug me—

bracelets and bangles jingling all the way. Stanley was a gay man—a hustler—trying to survive by selling his body. But he was a gentle soul, eager for friendship and acceptance. "I love you! I love you!" he would sing aloud as he hugged me. "I love you too, Stanley," I would smile as he beamed with delight. I always looked for Stanley and listened for the jangling of his cheap jewelry. He was a special and beloved character on the harsh and soulless streets.

But Stanley didn't appear for a couple of nights and apprehension rose within me . . . The newspaper report simply stated that Stanley was shot and killed by the police in a scuffle in a local tavern . . . Stanley. My gentle, lonely friend. Shot. Dead. There was no inquiry that I ever heard of. There was no autopsy. For Stanley was gay. He was black. He was a hustler. He was an outcast. He was impure. He was my friend. And I loved him.

You are black, my brother,
and my whiteness cries for you
for there won't be any shadow
without your rich, dark hue.
And I'll lose my way, my brother,
in a landscape stretched flat white
for there'll be no contoured valleys
without the shining of the night.

You are nameless, my sister,
and you leave me incomplete,
for I cannot know my fullest self
unless our two souls meet.
And I'll be bereft, my sister,
until we sing your name aloud
and you raise your head amongst us—
welcomed, celebrated, proud.

You are gay, my brother,
and a source of grace to me
reflecting on our human race
God's rich diversity.
And I need your courage, brother,
as you stand for who you are,
shining in our blindness
a lone and brilliant star.

WISDOM OF THE BROKEN

When Jesus saw the crowds, he went up the mountain; and after he sat down, his disciples came to him. Then he began to speak, and taught them, saying:

> *"Blessed are the poor in spirit, for theirs is the kingdom of heaven.*
> *Blessed are those who mourn, for they will be comforted.*
> *Blessed are the meek, for they will inherit the earth.*
> *Blessed are those who hunger and thirst for righteousness, for*
>   *they will be filled.*
> *Blessed are the merciful, for they will receive mercy.*
> *Blessed are the pure in heart, for they will see God.*
> *Blessed are the peacemakers, for they will be called children of God.*
> *Blessed are those who are persecuted for righteousness' sake, for*
>   *theirs is the kingdom of heaven."*

—MATTHEW 5:1-10

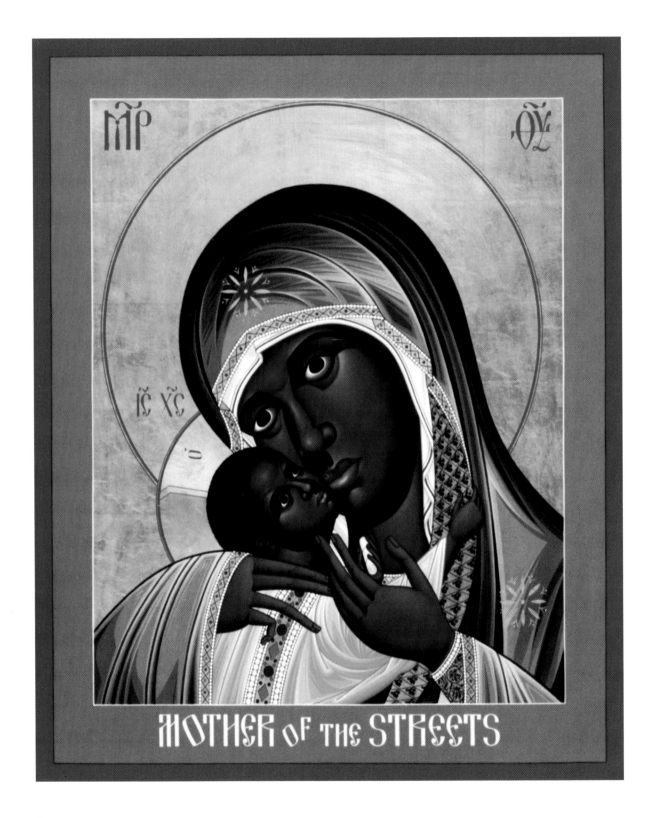

MOTHER of the STREETS

Mother of God:
Mother of the Streets

Each year larger numbers of homeless people live in the streets of our cities. These people may be jobless workers, battered women, the untreated mentally ill, or simply those too poor to get by. They tend to be invisible to the rest of society, but they are a real presence of Christ, the Suffering Servant, in history.

This icon depicts the Mother of God as the mother of those on the streets. Her garments, and those of her Son, are covered with jewels and gold decoration, manifesting the hidden worth and dignity of street people, who are living icons of God.

In 1984 the Catholic bishops of the United States declared, "To turn aside from those on the margins of society, the needy and the powerless, is to turn aside from Jesus. Such people show his face to the world." Such people are also a presence of Church, for where Christ is, there is his Church.

This icon hangs above the door of St. Boniface Church in the Tenderloin district of San Francisco. Franciscan friars who staff the church leave the doors open so that the homeless can come in to get warm.

Η ΑΓΙΑ ΡΟΔΗ

ST. ROSE of LIMA

Saint Rose of Lima
(1586-1617)

The life of this saint is like a rose among thorns. She was born into a poor but upper-class family in Peru soon after the conquest. As a child she suffered physical and psychological abuse from her neurotic mother and grandmother, each of whom slapped or beat her when she answered the name the other had given her—Isabel or Rose. After several years, when the bishop of Lima finally established that her name was Rose, the slaps and beatings stopped, but she could never please her mother.

Coming from such a bewildering childhood, she identified deeply with the suffering Christ. She longed to become a nun, but was prevented by her family from doing so. She practiced austere penances at home and eventually became a Dominican tertiary. She was a close friend of another Dominican saint with an unhappy childhood, Martin de Porres. To help support her family, she did fine embroidery and raised flowers for sale. Along with flowers, she raised medicinal herbs, which she used to cure the sick poor of Lima who began flocking to her small infirmary in her family's home. She had a special love and concern for the Indians who had been savagely conquered by men like Pizarro. She herself had Inca blood.

Her love for God was passionate and deep. She wrote mystical poetry that she occasionally sang with a guitar. Like many a Spanish mystic, she had to defend herself before the dreaded Inquisition. Near the end of her short life, a small bird came each day at sunset and sang with her a love song that she had composed. She died after a painful illness, just as a clock was striking midnight—reminiscent of the Gospel parable of the bridegroom and the ten virgins bearing lamps.

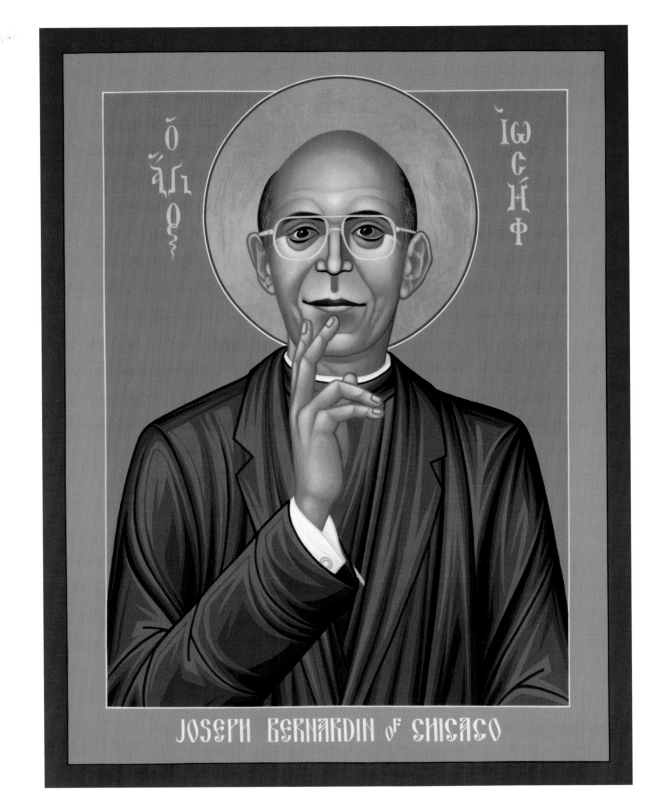

JOSEPH BERNARDIN OF CHICAGO

Cardinal Bernardin of Chicago
(1928-1996)

I've tried to create a climate in which people get along with each other. There are people at the extremes who are just as angry with me and the church now as they were when I came, but I think I've gotten people to accept each other a little bit better. I've given people permission to be themselves.

—JOSEPH CARDINAL BERNARDIN

When Cardinal Bernardin gave his first sermon as Archbishop of Chicago he announced, "I am your brother, Joseph." He always reached out to people on the margins like a brother, and lived in the margins of suspicion when accused of a crime he did not commit. When the cardinal forgave the man who admitted to falsely accusing him, he witnessed to the fundamental goodness in all of us. When "brother Joseph" died of cancer in 1996, he reminded us all how to live.

In this icon he gazes out at us as he did so often during his life, in the pose of one who listens—and one who listens well. It is not always easy to hear what the marginalized have to tell us. Their truth may be blurred by anger, slurred by pain, or whispered from insecurity or fear. When a person at the center, like Joseph Bernardin, makes the effort to listen to those at the margins, however, miracles happen and God's kingdom reappears.

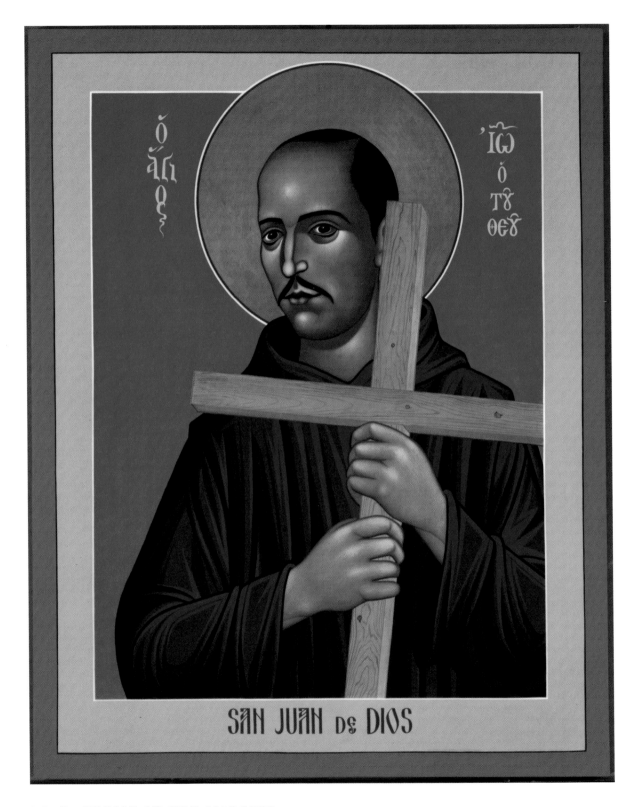

ὁ ἅγιος ᾿Ιω ὁ τῦ θεῦ

SAN JUAN DE DIOS

Saint John of God
(1495-1550)

In 1539 Granada, Spain, was a bustling city, growing ever more wealthy due to the exploits of the adventuresome explorers of the New World. However, as the rich became richer, the poor became poorer, more forgotten and ignored. The sick, the old, and the handicapped often were left in the gutter to die or to beg. Juan Ciudad, a man who would later be called "of God," went about the streets of Granada imploring all he met to "Do good to yourself by doing good for others." Hospitalized himself for what people imagined was a "mental breakdown," he discovered the redemptive value of suffering. Transformed by the experience, he labored for three years, unceasingly caring for those in the pain and anguish of suffering. He opened his own hospice and called it a "House of God."

"Remember Our Lord Jesus Christ and his blessed passion and recall how he returned good for the evil they did him," he would instruct. In the self-emptying Jesus Christ he saw the manifestation of a man who died to make us well. John of God understood that love has a healing and therapeutic value for those who are sick, dying, and abandoned by the systemic injustices of an economy that favored the rich, allowing the poor to become poorer. Relationships are healing and so he sought to restore human dignity to the ill and forgotten. While he poured his energy out in the service of others, the source of his energy was the crucified Christ.

John died at fifty-five years of age on March 8, 1550, of pneumonia, after he plunged into a river to save a young man from drowning. In 1690 he was canonized by Pope Alexander VII, and in 1886, Pope Leo XIII declared him the heavenly patron of all hospitals and the sick. He is also recognized as patron of nurses, booksellers, and firemen. He is the founder of the Hospitaller Brothers of Saint John of God, an order dedicated to the care of the sick and suffering.

ΗΑΓΙΑ ΠΕΡΠΕΤΥΑ

ΗΑΓΙΑ ΦΕΛΙСΙΤΑС

STS. PERPETUA AND FELICITY

Saints Perpetua and Felicity
(Killed March 7, 203)

Prisons have always broken those they have held. From the time of the Gospels, however, when Christ identified himself with those in prison, to our day of gulags and concentration camps, the Divine Mystery has often exploded into our world from these places at the margin.

Perpetua was a noble North African woman with an infant son. She was arrested with her pregnant slave Felicity because the two were Christians. Cutting through pious verbiage, we can say that the two young mothers were thrown into a filthy jail as prisoners of conscience. Perpetua's rich father tried to get her to compromise with the authorities, but her husband seems to have abandoned her completely in order to save his career. No one cared what happened to Felicity, except for Perpetua, whom prison was turning from mistress into friend.

The account of their martyrdom describes the misery they endured in prison, the anguish they felt when their children were taken from them, and the torture with wild animals that led to their deaths. Friendship and their deeply held beliefs were all that sustained them in that third-century detention center.

Millions of Perpetuas and Felicitys have perished at the hands of secret police, terrorist death squads, and national armies in the past hundred years. Some are famous like Victor Jara of Chile, Edith Stein of Auschwitz, or Padre Pro of Mexico. Others are known only to friends and family. Too many more have simply disappeared. Sometimes they have believed in the "wrong" God. Mostly they have resisted oppression, which means they have refused to allow God's image to be trampled in themselves and in others. They have been ripped from homes and loved ones and taken to dark places at society's margins to be destroyed. It is their torturers and murderers who eventually fall into oblivion, however, for the startling example of the marginalized victims lives on to inspire the rest of us. This book is dedicated to the Christ who is found at the margins of our world. Prisoners of conscience show us his crucified face and remind us that the cross is more than a pretty decoration. It is at the margins that we will find our faith.

REFLECTION *by Edwina Gateley*

Being broken is not something we naturally seek out as a condition to be embraced. On the contrary, we generally expend a great deal of time and energy ensuring that we maintain ourselves to the outward world as intact and secure as possible. Most of us make it our business to communicate ourselves as together, solid individuals, quite in control of our lives and our destinies, and not about to reveal any cracks or vulnerabilities that might damage our well-preserved public persona. Indeed, there are many in our world who have such self-discipline—or who are so far removed from their essential selves—that they maintain these false projections of themselves all their lives. Many never discover who they are at all.

Such a reality represents a great diminishment of the face of God on earth. But the risk of vulnerability is a great one. It is vulnerability that exposes the tender inner core of our humanity. When touched upon, both our awesome strengths and fragile weaknesses are revealed. Here, in this deep and silent place, dwells the grace of God. And here, in quiet moments, do we come to know that the fullness of our divinity is to be found in the fullness of our humanity. Each of us is essentially a wondrous mixture of earth and heaven, light and shadow, body and spirit, sin and sanctity and our life's journey is intended to lead us to embrace all of it and, ultimately to come to recognize the paradox of becoming whole and balanced through brokenness.

All those who have steadfastly pursued the life of the Spirit know what it means to wrestle with that part of our humanity that desires to stay in control and make us into little gods rather than break ourselves open and find that we are embraced and absorbed by the God who leaves us speechless and trembling.

It is the broken, freely choosing to say yes to God in the midst of their chaos, who become aware of such speechless trembling before the Divine. It is the Johns of God, the Roses of Lima, the Joseph Bernardins, the Perpetuas and the Felicitys who stand before God and before us, beautiful and whole in their brokeness. Their wisdom, born of suffering, shines on our horizons—inviting understanding, inviting us not to be afraid to die to all that which falsely leads us to imagine we are alive.

If we dare to say yes to deep authentic life, we present ourselves naked and expectant before the providence and compassion of God. Such a stance is not for the spiritually faint-hearted. The Divine Lover is no simpering gentle suitor, but One who will rather turn us upside down and shake all the restrained, pietistic nonsense out of us in search of a deep passionate love as we hear in the words of the great Sufi mystic and poet, Hafiz:

Love wants to reach out and manhandle us
Break all our teacup talk of God.
If you had the courage and
Could give the Beloved His choice, some nights,
He would just drag you around the room
By your hair,
Ripping from your grip all those toys in the world
That bring you no joy.
Love sometimes gets tired of speaking sweetly
And wants to rip to shreds
All your erroneous notions of truth
That make you fight within yourself, dear one,
And with others,
Causing the world to weep
On too many fine days.
God wants to manhandle us,
Lock us inside of a tiny room with Himself
And practice His dropkick.
The Beloved sometimes wants
to do us a great favor:
Hold us upside down
And shake all the nonsense out.
But when we hear
He is in such a "playful drunken mood"
Most everyone I know
Quickly packs their bags and hightails it
Out of town.

—"Tired of Speaking Sweetly"
in *The Gift—Poems by Hafiz.*

John of God, Rose of Lima, Joseph Bernardin, Perpetua and Felicity did not pack their bags and hightail it out of town. They stayed faithful and steadfast to the struggles of life and love, leaving behind for the rest of us their wondrous gift of courage.

At our first tentative and brave yes, God will begin to prise away from our grasp all that distracts us and deludes us from true relationship with the Divine. God so longs to fill us that, if we dare hunger for that fullness, much of what we cling to in our sad efforts to fill the spaces and the loneliness in our lives must ultimately give way to the priority of love and compassion. It is, of course, the classical notion of purification but much bolder and braver than the expressions of our past religious notions of sacrifice such as have been traditionally associated with Lenten observances of fasting, penance, and ritual. So in love with us is God that, given half a chance, God will indeed unashamedly haul the unsuspecting seeker into dark and passionate places of transformation.

Our icons in this chapter are just such unsuspecting seekers. They are dragged so deeply down into their humanity that they see the underside of God, and long, even in the midst of their struggles, to see the face of God. The divine encounter is a fierce and fiery thing that burns away all timidity and fear and leaves the lovers naked in their humanity, conscious only of being held in their fragility by the grasp of God.

Such a journey into one's deepest self is both frightening and liberating—frightening because it hurls us into a place we have not been before, liberating because we come to understand that all our trembling, all our brokenness, and all our dreams are held, along with us, in the palm of God's hand. It is the moment of faith. It is from such an awareness of God's immanence that true wisdom is born. And it is a speechless wisdom. It simply shines. It simply is. And we who observe such wisdom recognize it as coming from a deep place of anguish given over to God and washed in grace.

Some years ago, when I had been banned from speaking in many dioceses throughout the United States for the canonical infraction of wearing a stole that someone had placed upon me during a Eucharistic liturgy, I experienced myself as painfully rejected and silenced by the Church I had loved and served all my life. Bishop after bishop and parish after parish called or wrote to cancel my conferences. But one, Joseph Cardinal Bernardin of Chicago, responded differently. He had received calls and letters from a number of bishops asking for his opinion on this matter—given that I was a member of his diocese. Joseph Bernardin not only telephoned to talk to me personally, he also invited me to his residence not, he insisted, "to investigate or to censure, but to listen to your story. I want (he repeated) to listen to your story."

And so we met. The Cardinal's gentleness and compassion touched my heart as I shared my pain and rejection with him. I knew that the man who sat with me had suffered. I could see it in his eyes. What I did not know at the time was how much more broken he was to become before God scooped him up and took him home. But I saw and experienced before that time God's grace already richly present in Joseph Cardinal Bernardin. I sensed a connection with this man who knew about suffering and bore it with such gentle dignity. "You will always be welcome in my diocese," he whispered. In that time of approbation and censure, Joseph Bernardin reflected for me the grace

and compassion of God, the Wisdom of the Broken. I was deeply grateful.

How ironic it is that God often chooses to whisper to us through the lives of those who have lost their voice in our society, those who have no place, no credibility, no clout—those who are all broken up. Recently I facilitated a retreat for women in recovery from drugs and prostitution. The retreat was held in a Benedictine monastery, which welcomed them with traditional Benedictine hospitality. So humbled and grateful were these broken women, and so in awe of the reality of the sacred space in which they now found themselves, that one of them, in tears, shared how she felt: "God has tucked us up in bed with angels," she breathed in awe and disbelief. "Women like us, in the City of God—with *angels*!" Her eyes shone and she spoke as if she were in the center of a miracle. And indeed she was. *She* was the miracle. For she, from all her pain and the trauma and violence of her life, recognized and drank in the wondrous presence of God—articulating that wonder for the rest of us. Wisdom, indeed, from the broken. We simply wept at the naked vulnerability. And Mary, the Mother of the Streets, the Protectoress of the Oppressed—deeply present with us—smiled upon our little gathering.

No one knows what happened to John of God when he was eight years old. All that is known is that he disappeared from his loving family home and eventually turned up, a homeless child, at the other end of the country. Was he kidnapped? Abused? Did he run away himself? (Conventional wisdom assures us that happy and loved children do not become runaways.) Did he suffer from a mental disorder that drove him into temporary amnesia?

Whatever it was, the experience scarred him for life and left him eventually, as an adult, depressed and dissolute, culminating with an enforced stay in a mental institution. John suffered. John was broken. But he reached the point where that very experience, coupled with an ardent longing for God, led him, like Rose of Lima, to give his life to the sick, the outcasts, the dying, and the mentally ill. John of God knew what it was like to be there. He had been plummeted into his own brokenness and it left him with a desire to tend and heal the brokenness of others. His healing ministry has spanned hundreds of years through the work of his foundation, the Hospitaller Brothers of St. John of God.

The kind of empathy that spills out in such compassion and sacrifice for others is what will change us and our world. It is God's unceasing invitation to each one of us, no matter what burdens we bear, to allow compassion to flow through our broken places onto others who need to feel God's gentle kiss through the touch of our caring. We are not called to transcend our suffering—we are called to absorb it into compassion like Rose of Lima, John of God, and Joseph Bernardin.

We are ultimately called to absorb our compassion into God as did Perpetua and Felicity through the final giving of their lives. And somewhere, in their quiet and vulnerable moments, each one of these luminous spirits knew without a doubt that they were "tucked in bed with angels."

Holy Fools

But God chose what is foolish in the world to shame the wise; God chose what is weak in the world to shame the strong; God chose what is low and despised in the world, things that are not, to reduce to nothing things that are . . .

— 1 Corinthians 1:27-28

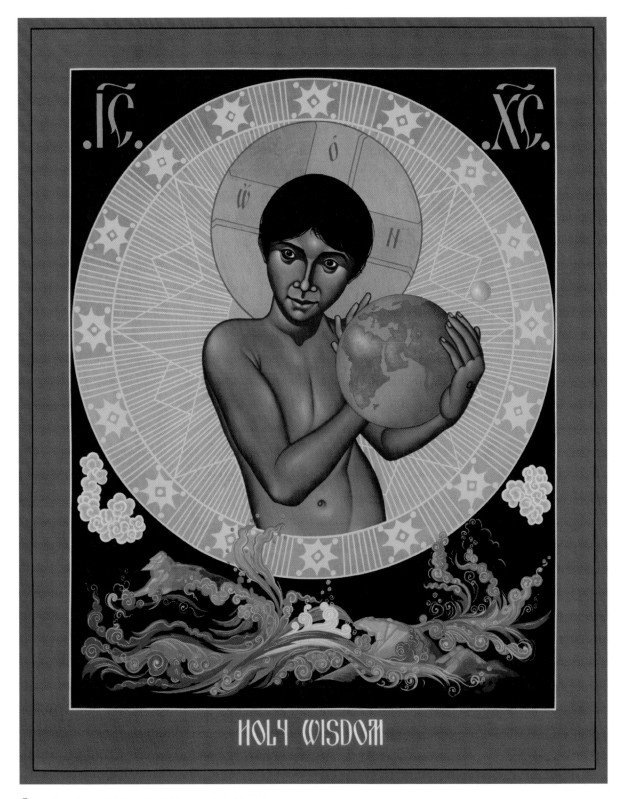

HOLY WISDOM

Holy Wisdom: Life-Giving Spring

Wisdom is bright, and does not grow dim.
By those who love her she is readily seen,
and found by those who look for her.
Quick to anticipate those who desire her, she makes herself known to them.
Watch for her early and you will have no trouble;
you will find her sitting at your gates.
Even to think about her is understanding fully grown;
be on the alert for her and anxiety will quickly leave you.
She herself walks about looking for those who are worthy of her
and graciously shows herself to them as they go,
in every thought of theirs coming to meet them.

—WISDOM 6:7-12

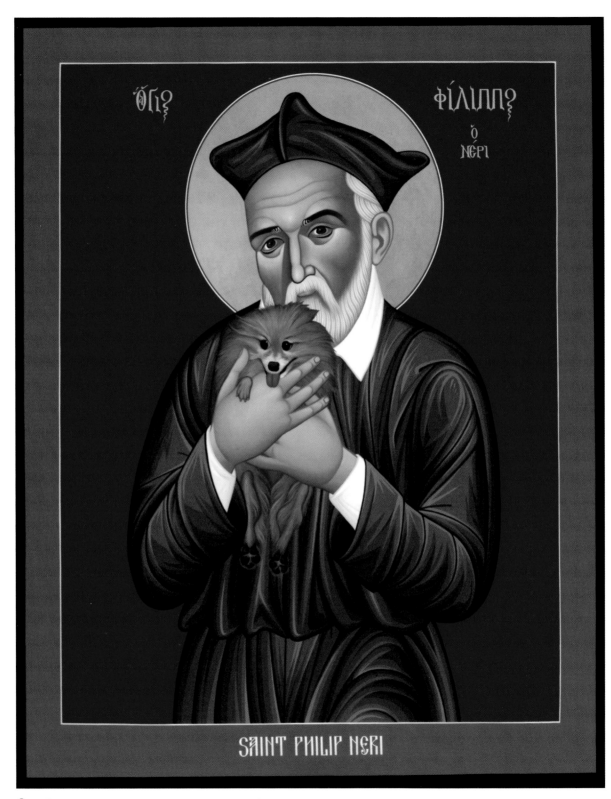

ὉΓΙꞶ ΦΊΛΙΠΠꞶ
Ὸ ΝΕΡΙ

SAINT PHILIP NERI

Saint Philip Neri
(1515-1595)

After a brief career in his native Florence, Philip Neri left the business world to pursue the spiritual longings of his heart in Rome. For seventeen years he lived a simple life, gathering other young men around himself to pray and to help pilgrims and the sick. At thirty-six he was ordained a priest and was soon renowned as a skillful spiritual director and confessor. In an oratory built at San Girolamo he continued his spiritual nurturing, sponsored religious lectures and discussions, organized work to help the suffering, and hosted performances of religious music, which evolved into what are now known as "oratorios." By 1575 he had formed the clergy who helped him in this work into the Congregation of the Oratory, a new form of Catholic religious life, whose members do not take the traditional vows.

Rome in Philip's day was in a very demoralized state. First as a layman and then as a priest, he and his companions worked to restore a vigorous spirituality among the people of Rome. He maintained that spiritual perfection was meant as much for lay people as for clergy and religious. He stressed love, gentleness, cheerfulness, and humility rather than physical austerity. In time he became known as the "Apostle of Rome."

Saint Philip is known more than most saints for his cheerfulness and his sense of humor. Like the "holy fools" of the Orthodox Church, he often resorted to unconventional behavior—such as shaving off half of his beard—in order to make a point. Many were shocked by such behavior. In this icon he is shown with a small dog he filched from one of the cardinals in Rome. Arrogant young aristocrats who came to him for guidance often found themselves walking this little dog—thus learning a bit of humility and sense of proportion. Philip Neri told jokes and appreciated laughter.

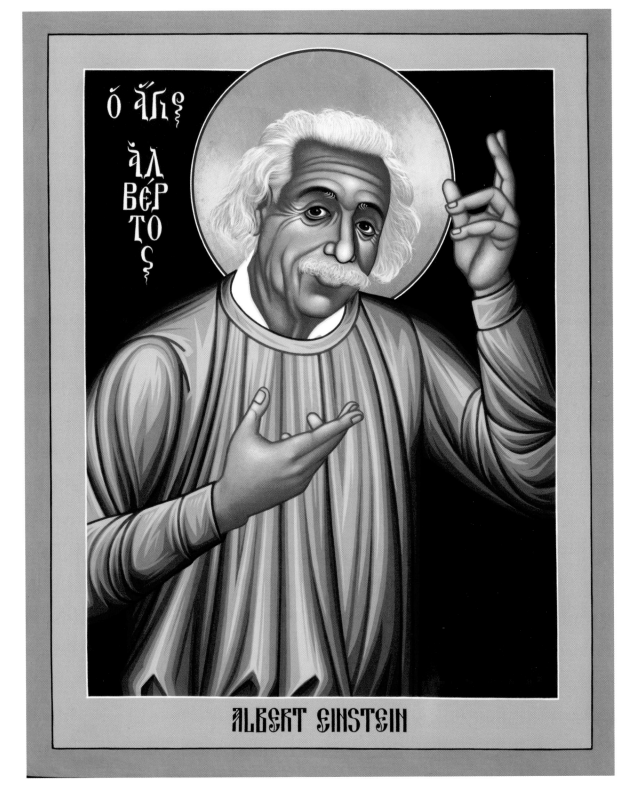

Ὁ ἅγιος ἈΛΒέΡΤΟΣ

ALBERT EINSTEIN

Albert Einstein
(1879–1955)

"It was not my rational consciousness that brought me to an understanding of the fundamental laws of the universe."

"The most beautiful experience we can have is mysterious."

"I want to know how God created this world. I am not interested in this or that phenomenon, in the spectrum of this or that element; I want to know his thoughts; the rest are details."

"More and more I come to value charity and love of one's fellow being above everything else . . . All our lauded technological progress—our very civilization—is like the axe in the hand of the pathological criminal."

"Small is the number of them that see with their own eyes and feel with their own hearts."

"Imagination is more important than knowledge."

"If I had it to do all over again, I'd become a plumber."

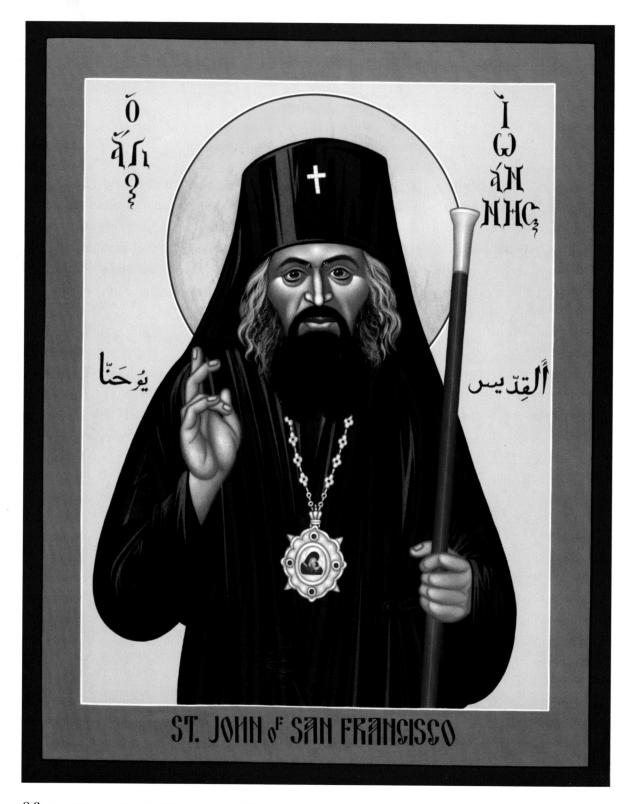

ST. JOHN of SAN FRANCISCO

Saint John of San Francisco
(1896–1966)

Archbishop John Maximovitch was born in southern Russia and fled with his family to Belgrade during the communist revolution. He taught in the orthodox seminary after he was ordained a priest-monk. He was consecrated bishop for the diocese of Shanghai and tended his flock there through the dangerous days of World War II. When the Russians fled from the communist takeover in China, he helped get almost all the refugees into the United States.

In 1951 he was appointed bishop in Western Europe, first in Paris and then in Brussels. The French remember him as "holy John the barefoot" since he never wore socks and often gave his sandals away to beggars. This was part of the behavior that marked him as a "holy fool," a special spiritual path in the Byzantine tradition. He gave little thought to his physical appearance, behaved in dramatic ways that sometimes embarrassed his peers, and barely slept or ate.

At the end of his life he became archbishop of San Francisco, where he had to bring peace to the contentious émigré community. He foretold the time and place of his death, and his body remained incorrupt after his death. He has been canonized by the bishops of his church.

Before all else Saint John was a man consumed with love. He was known during his lifetime as a clairvoyant with the power to heal through his prayers. Miracles continue to pour from his relics in the cathedral he built. The inscriptions on this icon are in English, Greek, and Arabic, bearing witness to his ability to recognize holiness wherever it found him.

ST. ANTHONY of PADUA

Saint Anthony of Padua
(1195-1231)

Anthony was born in Lisbon, Portugal. As a young man he joined the Augustinian Order, where he received an excellent education. At twenty-five, he received permission to transfer to the new Franciscan Order. Although he had hoped to work and die as a missionary in northern Africa, his poor health forced him to remain in Europe.

The Franciscans recognized his exceptional gift of preaching, and assigned him to areas in Italy where the Cathari and Waldensian sects were attracting many followers. Saint Francis knew him personally, and it was through Anthony's example of combining knowledge with humility and holiness that Francis allowed his other friars to pursue education.

Anthony was so interested in his work that he paid scant attention to his clothes, which often looked ragged. He also had a profound love for solitude, and, when traveling or preaching tours, he spent as much time in solitary prayer as his duties permitted. He often climbed trees to find solitude, and a benefactor built him a hermitage in a large walnut tree near the end of his life.

In spite of the many miles he walked, Anthony became quite fat in his last years. The day of his death, he suffered what may have been a stroke. At his own request, he was carried in an ox-cart for five or six hours to Padua. He died before reaching the city, but was buried there with great solemnity. He was canonized by the pope the following year.

While this doctor of theology may have seemed foolish to those who judge by appearances, Anthony is remembered as a great miracle-worker, both during his life and since his death. He is often pictured with the Christ child, who appeared to him one night before his death. He is particularly popular among the poor of the world, who have found in him a ready ear for their many needs.

REFLECTION *by Edwina Gateley*

St. Paul's admonition that we are to be "fools for Christ's sake" is demonstrated to its fullness in the lives of these extraordinary people—Saints Philip Neri and Anthony of Padua, Albert Einstein, and Archbishop John Maximovitch. The reality is that most of us have absolutely no desire whatsoever to be, or be considered as, remotely foolish. Rather we put much time and effort into coming across as eminently normal and acceptable. This, of course, is because we all, deep down, want to fit into society and not be the object of anyone's criticism or disapproval. One way or another, we are all into the business of wearing masks—respectable ones—that cover up any ideas or longings that might leave us on the fringes of what is acceptable and permissible, or that might leave us looking or speaking or acting differently from the norm. Such feelings, opinions or longings, if given expression, might well rock the polite and placid sensibilities of a church or society plodding along as safely and securely as possible and thereby keeping to the "letter of the law." Holy fools do not always keep to the letter of the law. They choose to be faithful to the holy wisdom within, refusing to compromise the spirit of truth.

Holy fools remind us of the richness and versatility of the human spirit. They challenge entrenched systems of narrow-minded thinking and oppression by living out their own truth and being utterly faithful to their inner calling in spite of the ridicule or even danger they may risk. Holy fools are the supreme witnesses to authenticity. Many of us aren't really sure what authenticity means today—it is so hard to be one's true self in a world so ordered and mediated by external powers (politicians, advertisers, media, corporations, etc.). We raise our children to conform for fear they will not otherwise fit into society. Children—who are born uniquely different and individual with particular gifts, talents and ways of perceiving—are soon knocked into shape by regimented school systems and constant messages that to be different is to be excluded. I became conscious of my unwitting participation in such a system when I urged my sturdy, extroverted, and sensitive then second grader not to take his well-loved and treasured doll to school. I wanted to protect him from ridicule in a society that stereotypes male and female roles and behaviors. Somewhat bewildered and disappointed, my son got the message. I was relieved. But at a deeper level I felt diminished and saddened. Conditioning to conformity begins early and leaves us as we grow, reluctant to follow our own star, rarely able to be our true selves and determined not to be fools.

In our efforts to keep up and do all the

things we seem to need to do, we gradually become part of the system itself, no matter how unjust it may be. God forbid that we should rock the system by not performing appropriately or by daring to be different and singing a different song! Yet something at a deeper level tells us that all is not well. We have lost sight of the bigger, multifaceted, and multicolored picture. Something disturbs us in the night or in the silence of a lonely moment. We long for something else, yet feel trapped in the relentless round of life's demands. So often we sadly proclaim that we have no choice but to plod on respectably and dutifully. Yet the fool and clown in us (if we are at all in touch with our inner selves) continues to stir beneath our well-learned and polite behaviors. We are, you see, meant to be as gods and goddesses. That in itself invites us to a different and radical perspective—we are called, as we read in Scripture, to fullness of life. Anything less than that is, at some level, whether we are conscious of it or not, going to leave us with a sense of loss or lack of meaning.

Not so for the holy fools who live on the margins of our world. They dare cry out loud and embarrassingly for authenticity right in the midst of conformity. They are ridiculous enough to respond to the spirit at the core of their being, which urges them to break out of any mold that would stifle their essential truth and vision. The holy fools are those who would declare aloud that the emperor has no clothes when everyone else is proclaiming how well and good he looks. The holy fools are those who trail up and down outside federal buildings carrying placards denouncing war or the death penalty or supporting some other

unpopular issue. The holy fools are those who lose their jobs because they question, or challenge, unjust employment practices. The holy fools are those who, driven to authenticity by being in touch with their inner truth and vision, risk reputation, employment, security, and even their lives in pursuit of what they believe is right. To the holy fool the greatest sin is conformity. For the most part, the rest of us stand by and smile, and our smile might well mask a longing to join their ranks were we foolish enough.

Like the prophets, visionaries, and mystics in our human story, God sends us holy fools to remind us of a different perspective, to nudge us into a passionate awareness of the inspiration and wonder of irreverence before our idols and our systems, and to dare us to dance to a different tune.

It would be well if indeed we dare to be fools in the sense of stepping out of line in the pursuit of truth and justice. Such daring acts of defiance would probably change the world as well as transform ourselves. We do not have to be lifetime fools—such a calling can be well left to the truly holy fools—but all of us are invited to be fools from time to time. All of us are aware of situations and events where we experience that stirring impulse within us to stand up and be counted for our Gospel values and therefore for our inner truth, or to ask the irreverent question.

Sometimes such impulses lead us to strange and different places. For me it was to spend nine months living in an old trailer in the woods without electricity or running water. Of course, from a rational point of view, it was a ridiculous thing to do. I had a degree in theology, there were all kinds of commendable and useful options before me. But I was driven to solitude and apparent unproductivity. As time went on and the months passed uneventfully and often boringly, I felt even more ridiculous. Why was I doing this? Who did I think I was? Why wasn't I doing something truly useful and beneficial (and therefore acceptable) in the world? I did not have the answer to superficial questions. I was following a deeper authenticity within myself, which, at that point, did not make sense even to my own rational thinking. I was, in reflection, being a holy fool, stepping out of line for a deeper truth and hunger, even though I did not at the time understand its meaning. Holy fools do not debate the reasons for, or the possible consequences of, their actions—they do what they know they must, they are who they know they must be. What follows as a consequence of their unconventional behavior is left in the hands of God.

For me it was a deepening awareness of my call to minister with women on the streets. It was not a call I could have even begun to hear if I had not stayed in the forest long enough to hear God's whisper. Indeed, had I not been fool enough to spend all my savings on a battered trailer and sit in it feeling useless and inconsequential for nine months, I would never eventually have opened a safe and healing home for women from the streets. When we step out of line in pursuit of what is a profound sense of rightness, we open the way for new and amazing revelations of the work of God's grace in the world.

Jesus, of course, was the ultimate holy fool. Utterly refusing to be bought by the political and religious system of his time, he was faithful to the call of compassion and justice deep within his soul—putting that and his own integrity before all else. In a patriarchal and macho society, Jesus did not hesitate to allow his true feelings to be expressed, weeping aloud over Jerusalem and letting out "a great wail" before the tomb of his friend Lazarus. In a hierarchically structured system, he welcomed the children and befriended women and outcasts; in the face of strict religious ethics and rituals that excluded the "impure," Jesus sat and ate and drank with sinners. He was fool enough, as John Maximovitch was hundreds of years later, to seek out and honor every single person as a reflection of God. Such pursuit of truth, in a society which has lost its way and given itself over to being less than human, is indeed a sign of a holy fool. But the fact that the systems and structures in which we find ourselves are flawed and often downright evil, does not necessarily mean that those systems or institutions themselves must be abandoned. Marginality within a system may ultimately help shift the whole system—like leaven in bread—into a different shape. But usually it is a lot easier to opt out rather than make an idiot out of oneself by standing up and yelling "foul!" in the midst of the gathered assembly.

Yelling "foul," however, is exactly what we may have to do. When a system or institution of any kind does not empower or liberate people towards fullness of life, then the holy fools of our world must, by whatever means are available to them, go against that system by refusing to participate or to conform. Most of us, fortunately, are not in a position (yet) where we have to put our very lives on the line as Anthony of Padua and Philip Neri did. Such a dramatic commitment to the Gospel through nonconformity will not be demanded of most of us. But all of us need to honestly look at where and how we have conformed to diminishment and inauthenticity, and where, in subtle and almost indiscernible ways, we have become dishonest and thereby prostituted our divine calling. When have we bought into systems less than liberating? Where have we compromised our essential honesty in order to be acceptable? It is often the holy fools right in our midst—those who are marginalized within our own families and institutions—who reveal to us our small and narrow visions. Frank did that for me.

Frank was a candidate for the Volunteer Missionary Movement that I was running. The VMM is a program to finally select and prepare men and women to work in villages and grassroots projects in developing countries. But Frank didn't look right. In fact, he never looked right. He should never have even got this far in our program, I thought, with some irritation. Frank's faded jeans were frayed in the legs, his shirt was always crumpled as if it had been rolled into a ball; his buttons were mostly not fastened and, to complete the picture of disorder, Frank wore a necklace and bangles!

"Frank," I protested one day, "you'll have to do something about yourself. You can't go around looking like . . . that."

"Why not?" responded Frank, appearing genuinely upset. "They're only clothes."

"Well—yes—I know that, but they're not right . . . You have to look better than that . . . If you want to go to Africa with our program you are going to have to take your necklace and bangles off . . . And you must fasten your buttons . . ." I trailed off feeling somewhat awkward.

"You want me to fasten my buttons?" Frank asked, wide eyed. "Yes, that's right," I answered defensively. "And take those bangles off. You can't be one of our missionaries wearing bangles . . . And you'll need to get your hair cut . . . Okay?"

Frank stared at me—gently defiant: "If I fasten my buttons, take off my bangles, and get my hair cut, you'll let me go to Africa," he said with a slight smile.

"Yes, you've got it," I answered righteously.

Frank did what had been asked of him. He began to look like the rest of the group, though there was something indefinable about him that still left me feeling that he was different—that he would never quite fit in. I was very tempted to reject Frank but in the end I allowed myself, reluctantly, to take the risk. Frank was sent to a remote village in East Africa. I prayed he (and the people) would survive.

They not only survived Frank, they loved him. I was inundated with letters from the mission thanking me for sending such a fine and dedicated young man to live and work with them! Frank was a spectacular success. The people loved him so much that Frank stayed over six years with them. The priests in charge of the mission told me that Frank was the best lay missionary that they had ever had, he had learned the local language and fitted in easily with the local people, whom he truly respected and loved.

Eventually he became a religious brother and continued working with the very poor. He

wrote to me telling me (I knew with a smile)
that he now had no buttons at all to fasten—
and he *always* wore his beads. Frank—holy
fool—left me humbled and a little bit wiser.

Holy fools!
Refusing to be constrained
by published creed and code,
daring to pour
brilliant blobs of color
on the neat black and white
of soul-less bureaucracy
and corporate power.

Holy fools!
Challenging small minds
and dried-up spirits

to quicken with forbidden fruit
and burst the narrowed vision,
laying bare
in awesome display
ultimate integrity.

Holy fools!
Breaking the rules
in the name of God
and refusing to recite the law
in favor of the spirit;
breaking down the prisons,
opening forbidden doors
to sing and dance to
a different
and most glorious tune.

Magic on the Margins

Let the same mind be in you that was in Christ Jesus, who, though he was in the form of God, did not regard equality with God as something to be exploited, but emptied himself, taking the form of a slave, being born in human likeness. And being found in human form, he humbled himself and became obedient to the point of death—even death on the cross.

Therefore God also highly exalted him and gave him the name that is above every name, so that at the name of Jesus every knee should bend, in heaven and on earth and under the earth, and every tongue should confess that Jesus Christ is Lord, to the glory of God the Father.

—Philippians 2:5-11

95

ὁ ἅгιος ΔΑΜΙΑΝὸς ὁ ΛΕΠΡός

OUR LORD PERMITS US NOW AND THEN TO PICK A BEAUTIFUL ROSE AMONG SHARP THORNS

DAMIEN THE LEPER

Damien the Leper
(1840-1889)

Damien de Veuster volunteered to go as a missionary to Hawaii when he was twenty-three years old. Blessed with physical strength, he was also a skilled carpenter. Each place he was assigned on the islands, he built churches, sometimes even hewing the wood from jungle trees. He traveled great distances on foot to celebrate Mass whenever he found new converts. After nine years of this work he volunteered once again to go away—this time to live with the lepers on Molokai.

Leprosy was one of Europe's many legacies to Hawaii. In Damien's day the disease was enshrouded by ignorance and was seen as a punishment from God—not unlike AIDS in our day. Lepers were torn from their families and quarantined on a rocky coast of Molokai. Once there, they could never leave. They lived in abject poverty, with no medical attention, surrounded by despair. By volunteering to be their parish priest, Damien cut himself off from the rest of the world.

On Molokai he built a church and homes for the lepers. He brought music back to them and encouraged them to sing. He painted his buildings bright colors. He ate with the lepers and shared their life. He personally dug graves for those who died. He fought with the government for better conditions. In time he, too, contracted the disease. To his bishop he wrote, "I am calm and resigned and very happy in the midst of my people."

By the time he died, Damien's efforts among the lepers had borne fruit. They lived in dignity, with better food and medical attention. Another priest had come to take Damien's place, as had an energetic layman and a group of Franciscan nuns. His death forced the Western world to re-examine leprosy, as well as its attitude toward the disease. Today many see him as a patron saint for those who have AIDS. Magic on the margins happens when someone "with eyes to see" looks at his brother or sister and sees the face of Christ.

Ο ΑΓΙΟΣ ΦΡΕΔΕΡΙΚΟΣ Ο ΟΖΑΝΑΜ

FRÉDÉRIC OZANAM

Frederic Ozanam
(1813-1853)

Antoine Frederic Ozanam was a French historian and literary scholar who founded the Society of Saint Vincent de Paul. As a teenager he went through a crisis of doubt, which he overcame with the help of a teacher, Abbe Noirot. This experience provided him with an intellectual foundation for his faith, which became characteristic of him for the rest of his life. While still a student, he began a series of refutations of new socialist doctrines and defended the position of the Catholic Church. With other students, he founded the Society of Saint Vincent de Paul, in order to assist the poor of every religion and nationality. This society continues to serve those on the margins throughout the world and has always kept its lay character.

In this icon Ozanam points to Christ in a sphere of glory on his breast. This is the Christ that Jesus described in Matthew 25, one of the least of the brethren. The vision of the various religious families connected with Saint Vincent de Paul is that Christ is best found where he is hardest to recognize—in the poor and downtrodden of the world. It is a vision that informs the best of Christian tradition, stretching from St. Martin of Tours to Mother Teresa of Calcutta. It is the vision of Georges Bernanos, Graham Greene, Georges Rouault, and Shusaku Endo. It is a subtle melody that lies beneath the baroque splendor of Rome and the complexities of Canon Law. For this vision one might become a holy fool, a great mystic, an inspired artist, or a prophet-martyr. Logic is turned on its head. Splendor shines forth from the mud. Here is an alchemy that truly works, a magic that never fails!

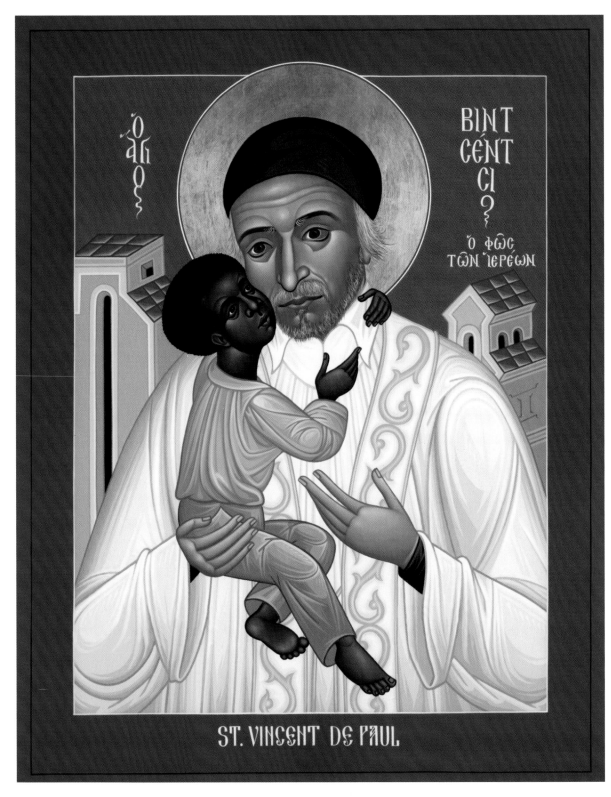

ST. VINCENT DE PAUL

Saint Vincent de Paul
(1580-1660)

For Saint Vincent de Paul becoming a priest meant escaping his family's poverty into a life of clerical ease. His first ten years as a priest were spent basking in his newfound comfort and privileges. Then a great change came over him and he eventually dedicated the rest of his life to the service of the poor. He organized groups of lay people for charitable work, and a society of priests who would train the clergy as well as do missionary work in rural areas. Today his name is synonymous with Catholic charity throughout the world.

Charity for Saint Vincent was not an impersonal gift of money. Each poor person was a sacramental presence of Christ and was to be revered. "The poor are your masters," he told his followers, "and you are their servants." Such a statement in the France of Louis XIV was revolutionary if not insane. "If you hear the poor calling you, mortify yourselves and leave God for God," he advised sisters who asked what to do when the doorbell rang during community prayer. "A Sister may go to the sick ten times a day, and ten times a day she will find God there."

Respect for every poor person was based not only on theology, but also on psychology. Assistance can either uplift or degrade a person, depending on how it is given. With great insight he said, "The poor will forgive you for giving them bread, only because of your love." The poor were no less human than the aristocrats at Versailles were, and their feelings were every bit as important.

In this icon Saint Vincent holds a black child in his arms, since poverty so often has dark skin in our times. Icons may contain anachronisms when there is a greater truth at stake. The Greek inscription reads, "Saint Vincent, the Light of Priests."

ΗΑΓΙΑ ΛΟΥ ΗС

ST. LOUISE DE MARILLAS

Saint Louise de Marillac
(1591-1660)

Louise de Marillac was the illegitimate daughter of a French nobleman. Although he provided for her and loved her dearly, he died when she was thirteen years old—leaving her at the mercy of relatives who withheld her inheritance. She married when she was twenty-two, and was widowed twelve years later.

Louise was a close friend of Saint Vincent de Paul. After the death of her husband, Vincent asked Louise to visit the nobility, encouraging them to greater generosity to the poor and correcting societal abuses.

Eventually a group of simple village women gathered around Louise. Together they became the Daughters of Charity, a new form of religious life dedicated to serving the poorest of the poor. Prior to this time, Catholic nuns had lived a life of strict seclusion in monasteries. The dream of Vincent and Louise was to take consecrated life into city streets. These new sisters performed spiritual alchemy: for monastery, they would have the house of the sick . . . for chapel, the parish church . . . for cloister, the streets of the city or the wards of the hospitals. They cared for the great numbers of abandoned orphans, for the aged poor, for prisoners, and for the sick. They started schools for poor children. They transformed the character of Christian charity by establishing permanent institutions to put charitable works on a stable footing.

At the heart of Christianity is a belief that Christ is best served in the poor. Louise reminds us of this truth as wealth becomes concentrated in ever fewer hands in our day. Her dying words to her sisters are words Christians must never forget: "Take great care to serve the poor."

Ό ΆΓΙΟΣ   ΜΙΧΆΗΛ

FATHER MYCHAL JUDGE

Mychal Judge, O.F.M.
(1933–2001)

As Muslim extremists flew highjacked commercial jets into the towers of the World Trade Center on September 11, 2001, they screamed, "God is great!" to complete their act of self-chosen "martyrdom." Thousands of innocent people were killed, people of many nationalities and different walks of life. The first official casualty was an elderly Franciscan priest who had just administered the last rites to a fireman who had been struck by the body of a woman who had jumped from the towers. His name was Mychal Judge and he was chaplain of the fire department.

The Koran begins with the words, "In the name of God most beneficent, most merciful." Most world religions proclaim God's mercy and compassion. The word martyr comes from the Greek word for witness. Mychal Judge was a true "martyr" who died bearing witness to God's mercy and beneficence, after a long life spent the same way.

Fr. Mychal Judge was a devoted priest who wore his Franciscan habit almost everywhere and rejoiced in his vow of poverty. The holy foolishness of the first Franciscans and their magical simplicity weaves in and out of the story of his life. As a priest he often sought out and comforted people who had been rebuffed by the harshness of other priests. His chief ministries were to the firemen of New York City, to recovering alcoholics in AA (of which he was one), to people suffering from AIDS, and to Franciscans preparing to make their solemn vows. When church authorities urged a boycott of the first gay-inclusive St. Patrick's Day parade in Queens, Mychal showed up in his habit and went out of his way to be interviewed by reporters. He once told an angry monsignor in the chancery who frequently called to admonish him, "If I've ever done anything to embarrass or hurt the church I love so much, you can burn me at the stake in front of St. Patrick's."

The word "martyr" has been twisted out of shape in the twenty-first century as religious extremists throughout the world try to impose their version of God's will. This joyful Franciscan friar reminds us of the stuff of which martyrs are really made and challenges us to witness to God's compassion, however mad our world may seem.

REFLECTION *by Edwina Gateley*

They leave us awestruck, these amazing figures of integrity who were so committed to truth and authenticity that they left their comfortable centers of existence to find fullness of life—and magic—on the margins. Imbued with a deep hunger for meaning they pursued it relentlessly—each step taking them further from their traditional and institutionalized comfort zones until, ultimately, they experienced the total stripping away of all that clouded and distorted their vision of God and the essential interconnectedness of all humanity. Their journeys speak of the seduction of the Holy Spirit who leads those who hunger and thirst for fullness of life along ways far beyond our understanding. We are often baffled by the eternal paradox of dying that we might live, of letting go and emptying out that we might be filled. But such a paradox is at the heart of the Christian message. Damien, Frederic Ozanam, Vincent de Paul, Louise de Marillac and Fr. Mychal Judge lived that paradox and, in doing so, left for us a legacy that forever stands to remind us that our own journeys are far from over and may begin again and again at any time. The invitation to discover the magic on the margins is always before us.

We are all called, ultimately, to wholeness and holiness, and that insistent urge for fullness resides within each one of us. We cannot, however, become whole whilst we experience ourselves as separate (physically, mentally, or emotionally) from the anawim—the poor and the disenfranchised. Although many people have an opportunity to live on the margins through their work with the marginalized, it is those who allow themselves to be transformed by them who are truly the icons of a new interconnected vision of the world. The very survival of our planet is dependent on such transformation and vision.

We are all affected by diminishment and poverty whether we see it or not, are conscious of it or not. At some unconscious level we too are diminished—and we know it. Something is missing, something is not right, and we feel restless in that empty space. St. Augustine said that we are made for God and our hearts are restless till they rest in God. I would add that our hearts are restless until all God's people live in peace and have access to the basic necessities of life. We will all know woundedness until we heal our world, for all is connected. Whether we recognize it yet or not, we are all interdependent. We are one body—our whole planet one living, breathing, multifaceted glorious creation of God. Our icons on the margins became conscious of that reality. As they immersed themselves in the poor and the marginalized, they were fed on a deeper level—they were nourished and transformed by the very wounded to whom they were sent.

Most of us, thank God, are not called to live on the extreme margins of society in order to be faithful. But all of us, at various points in our lives, are called to step out in pursuit of integrity and justice. When we do take such timid yet brave steps we may be sure that our souls will be stretched and we will see a little clearer as our horizons are widened. The process is always somewhat painful—stretching often is—but if we are not to be seduced into becoming part of an unjust system, we must be open to seeing more clearly and living more deeply than we often do. Our relatively comfortable lifestyles can leave us disconnected to what is really going on in the rest of our world. Understandably we probably don't really want to know what's going on anyway—we are aware that all is not well. News of famines, disasters, and real and imagined threats break unbidden into our suburban lifestyles. We are well aware that the whiff of evil is never very far away. Given that reality, and in spite of the faith that calls us to be fearless in the pursuit of truth and justice, it is tempting to simply hunker down and hold onto whatever bit of security and comfort we can. Rather than confronting the shadows of our world we are seduced into an apathy that leads us to deny the truth and to hide beneath those very shadows—thus becoming, ourselves, part of the world's darkness.

The alternative to denial is very disturbing. But we have to be disturbed until the Realm of God becomes a reality. We cannot but respond when the restless grace of God moves in our guts, stirring us to be vulnerable to conversion—to the stretching that carries us forward in the pursuit of truth and love. Even in the midst of our anesthetized lifestyles—especially in that very environment of relative comfort and safety—we are never without an invitation to be more than we elect to be. Those who choose to live on the margins beckon us to reject the lie of individualism and self-satisfaction and listen to the deeper calling within.

The very thing that disturbs and challenges us will likely be the catalyst for conversion and transformation leading to deeper insights, wisdom, and, ultimately, joy. Damien found his deepest joy in community with the most despised and abandoned of his time; Mychal served the gay community; and Louise de Marillac and Vincent de Paul came to deeper insight in working with the very poor. We will indeed discover something of the magic that Damien, Louise, Frederic, Vincent de Paul, and Mychal came upon that changed and transformed their lives and led them to give themselves totally to their brothers and sisters. Those whom we meet on the margins will lead us to a new understanding of the presence and wonder of God's grace in action in our world. The magic that we experience is the magic of the Spirit at work in us revealing our amazing capacity for transformation in the face of overwhelming odds. For only on the margins can one directly experience the interconnectedness of all humanity. We allow ourselves, then, to remove the barriers of race, color, class, or any illusion of separation. By walking with the marginalized we threaten our patriarchal system and witness to a new vision of human solidarity and interdependence. The person on the margins has a much clearer vision precisely by choosing the margins and being open to their magic. I know something about that because I have visited the margins, and I have encountered their miracles that have fed my soul and blessed me with a new and surer vision.

I met Sandy on the margins. One didn't get too close to Sandy. She had a scary reputation. In spite of her youth (she was still a teenager when I met her) her eyes, wary and suspicious, betrayed years of anger and hardship. There was no discernible trace of tenderness in this leader of one of the city's most violent female gangs. Everyone she encountered was a potential enemy—including myself.

I was naturally cautious with Sandy—not wishing to intrude into the space she had cast around herself for protection. What could have happened, I mused, to make this child so volatile and so angry at the world? Sandy had her "man" on the streets and everything she earned from her lifestyle of prostitution went to him. She cared for him and protected him as fiercely as a mother her child—even when he was jailed for murder. Sandy was devastated and desperately defended her man. The whole world, she believed, conspired against them. Her loyalty was total and uncompromising. Every week, in blinding snow or sweltering heat, she journeyed hours to visit him carrying whatever goodies she knew would please him.

One day, after years of slowly moving closer to my fierce little friend, she shared with me the violence done to her by her mother throughout her childhood—how she had been beaten, tied up, and told that she was hated. "But," Sandy added reflectively, "she's still my mom, isn't she?" This young woman's love, I thought, is utterly forgiving.

Suddenly one morning Sandy declared that it was her mother's birthday and that she want-ed to visit her and take her a gift. Would I drive her to her mother's apartment? I agreed but with some apprehension. That morning Sandy went out shopping. She came back—eyes shining—clutching a single red rose in a glass vase. "For my mom," she announced proudly. "And don't touch it!" she added warn-ingly to everyone within earshot.

The rest of the day Sandy fidgeted. She couldn't sit still or stay in one place for more than a few minutes. She constantly checked her watch for the time we had agreed to set off for her mother's home.

We drove through the city streets. Sandy, stroking the rose petals, was visibly nervous. Her hands were shaking. "She's my mom," she kept repeating. "I'm so scared." So was I. I tried to imagine what it must be like to be Sandy—desperate for love and security against all the odds. I so much wanted to protect her . . . We arrived at the apartment block where her mother lived. Sandy almost fell out of the car with excitement and began to walk rapidly towards the building. Then she slowed visibly and slowly walked back to me. "I'm scared," she repeated. "I hope she'll recognize me." Sandy was still shaking.

"It's O.K.," I said unconvincingly, and put my arm around her as we walked up to her mother's door. The place looked dead and derelict. Sandy rang the doorbell. And again. And again. "Must be out," she mumbled, loos-ening her grip on the rose. "Let's check next door," I said without enthusiasm. The neighbor, unkempt and unshaven, responded to Sandy's nervous enquiry: "She don't live 'ere anymore. Been gone about six months."

As we slowly walked away from the last known address of her mother, Sandy's body crumpled and she broke into heartrending sobs that came from some deep place within her and seemed to span all the years of her young life. All the way back home she sobbed a lifetime of pain and rejection. "I love her," she sobbed, as she tore the rose into shreds. "I'll always love her even though she hates me."

Sandy never married. She continued to visit her man in jail declaring her loyalty to him for life. "I'll always love him," she said, "even if he's in jail forever."

Over the years, Sandy worked desperately hard to get a good job and to pass exams that she had missed because of skipping school. Slowly and with amazing determination she plodded on until she had a steady job, her own apartment, and a car. "Now," declared Sandy one day, "now I'm going to adopt three kids from group homes." I was astounded. "That's crazy!" I responded. "Far too much to take on." "No," Sandy answered firmly. "I can do it. It's what I want to do because if somebody had done that for me—if somebody had given me a home and loved me—I would never have gone to the streets."

There was no dissuading Sandy. There was no stopping her. Hardly settled herself and still struggling to survive, Sandy fostered and then adopted three young children. I could only stand in apprehension, yet reluctant admiration, at such amazing—almost irresponsible—determination and unselfishness. I was awed by such powerful love that seemed to rise from nowhere and endured through so much. Sandy, who had never been loved or nurtured, drew from a reservoir of compassion deep within herself which left me astounded and awed by the power of God's grace. Sandy, the runaway,

homeless street girl, Sandy who was never mothered, never loved, gave the homeless a home, and she loved them. Fiercely.

Sandy's indomitable spirit, which broke through from the midst of violence and created miracles, will never cease to feed my soul in times of hopelessness and despair. The magic that her fierce love wrought on the edges of society has changed the world, and my own perceptions of that world. It has taught me to believe in the impossible and the improbable, and to draw on that belief in my work with those who experience themselves as beyond help or transformation.

On the margins one encounters people who are truly dependent on God and on each other. The Gospel is revealed in the way the marginalized care for each other, are naturally generous and live out of desperation a curious kind of inter-connectedness. This is what is magical in the encounter—they often know and experience God and the Gospel more directly and intimately than those of us in the mainstream. Late one night I did not have to venture far to encounter such a reality. Walking down a busy street, I was passing a huge old church. Parked at the bottom of its steep and worn concrete steps were three shopping carts piled high with plastic bags full of trophies and bits of junk collected from the streets and the garbage dumpsters. Five elderly, homeless women (known as shopping bag ladies) had arranged themselves on the church steps—one at the top and two on each edge of the next two steps going downwards. In the center they had placed a large plastic bottle of ginger ale surrounded by some cookies (smuggled, no doubt, from the nearby soup kitchen) and some styrofoam cups from McDonalds. The time was almost midnight. I hesitated on my walk and looked up at the unlikely gathering.

"We're having a picnic," yelled one of the women above the sound of a passing car. "Come and join us!" I did. Sitting on the bottom step I was given a napkin and a cup of ginger ale, then a cookie was decorously passed from hand to hand towards me. It had traveled far—like the ladies themselves.

Night fell. The traffic thinned out. Gradually the ladies ceased to chatter and to laugh. We all knew it was time to sleep. But there was nowhere to sleep. Along with the silence, a deep, deep, loneliness fell upon our little party. And in me arose a deep shame for the rich country in which I lived, a country that could not share its multiple resources with the very poor even as these very poor shared with me the little they had. How much more clearly the poor can live in solidarity and give us a vision of a new way of being. They had not hesitated to invite me to their party; their fare was meager, but their hearts—broken open— were large enough to invite me in. There was magic on the margins that cold, damp night. Through Sandy and the homeless women who shared their midnight picnic with me, I myself was drawn into the ranks of the marginalized. For to choose the margins leaves one in a different place than before. One's own social identity shifts and changes as one experiences and becomes part of a new and transforming reality. That reality is compassion. True compassion is not about being at one with one's own social cultural group, but it is being able to see and know oneself as connected to every human person without reservation. The words of Jesus, "I am in you and you are in me," become gloriously real and alive on society's edges. That experience itself is the magic on the margins.

Wisdom lured me
from my warm bed,
coaxing away
my blankets of security,
dispelling my dreams,
and whispering me
to tiptoe into darkness.

Wisdom opened the door
into the night.
rushing me round
with sharp cold air,
assailing my slumbering senses
with city noise and smells.

Wisdom guided me round
broken bottles and garbage,
urging me on
through a wilderness
of concrete despair.

Wisdom led me
past uncaring traffic,
to her holy place,
her gathering of friends and sisters,
who beckoned me to join
their midnight celebration.

Wisdom shared with me
a feast of love and kindness,
dispensing with joy
the Eucharistic banquet
lit up by the street lights
and the magic
on the margins.

Visionaries and Mystics

Come then, my love,

my lovely one, come.

My dove, hiding in the clefts of the rock,

in the coverts of the cliff,

show me your face,

let me hear your voice;

for your voice is sweet

and your face is beautiful.

—Song of Songs 2:13-14

CHRIST SOPHIA

Christ Sophia

The Jewish Scriptures use various names for God. "Wisdom" is among the names used most frequently, and God is always feminine when called Wisdom. "She is a reflection of the eternal light, untarnished mirror of God's active power, image of his goodness" (Wisdom 7:26). It is Wisdom who creates and orders the world, making manifest the divine will. And it is Wisdom who delights to be among the human race, teaching us her ways. Wisdom is the source of vision.

In the Byzantine Church, these references to Wisdom are considered references to Christ. Churches like Hagia Sophia in Istanbul are dedicated to Christ. From the Middle Ages on, icons depicting Christ as an androgynous figure, flanked by Mary and John the Baptist, have been painted in Russia and elsewhere. It is important now to take the next step and depict Wisdom—Sophia—as the woman sacred Scriptures describe.

Looking honestly at our ancient tradition, it is clear that the mystery of Christ cannot be described in masculine terms alone. Because of historical and cultural circumstances, the Second Person of the Trinity became a male human being. Before the Incarnation, however, that person was described as "she." As the Incarnation continues to unfold after Christ's resurrection and ascension, it is again the feminine Sophia who expresses the mystery—as pointed out by the Russian theologian Soloviev.

Christ Sophia is depicted in this icon in an egg-shaped mandala. The inscription in her halo is Greek for " I am who am," the divine name told to Moses at the burning bush on Sinai. The Greek inscriptions in the upper corners are abbreviations for "Jesus Christ," her historical manifestation. She holds the ancient statue called "Venus of Willendorf," and points to herself as if to say, "I am she. Know me more fully."

BLACK ELK

Black Elk
(1863-1950)

When he was nine years old, Black Elk, the great Oglala holy man, was shown a magnificent vision by the sacred Thunder-beings of the West, which changed his life. He was taken up into the heavens and given powers to heal and protect his people. He was also shown glimpses of their future. He was charged with their welfare and given a symbolic red staff to plant in their midst and bring to life. The vision took on universal qualities. "And I saw that the sacred hoop of my people was one of many hoops that made one circle, wide as daylight and as starlight, and in the center grew one mighty flowering tree to shelter all the children of one mother and one father."

Several years later he was present at the Battle of the Little Big Horn. In 1886 he joined Buffalo Bill's Wild West Show so that he could learn more about white people and their ways. His travels with Buffalo Bill in Europe had a lasting impression on him. In 1889, he returned to his tribe and the following year survived the slaughter at Wounded Knee.

Although he became a Roman Catholic and even worked with the Jesuit missionaries as a lay catechist, his vision and its responsibilities continued to haunt him. The missionaries insisted that he abandon the traditional religion of his people, but in his old age he collaborated with two Anglo-American writers to record the sacred rites of the Lakota, and his own life and shamanic vision. He grieved that he had never been able to care for his people as he had been charged—to bring the sacred red staff to life—and asked to be taken to Harney Peak in the Black Hills so that he could pray for this once more.

In this icon, the Thunder-beings are depicted as flaming eyes, for they have no bodies, but only eyes from which bolts of lightning flash. They are spirits who purify the earth. Black Elk is praying for the earth and its people with his sacred pipe. The red staff, planted in the great hoop which is our planet, has brought forth its first leaf as a symbol of life and hope.

ΗΑΓΙΑ ΙΥΛΙΆΝΑ

JULIAN OF NORWICH

Blessed Julian of Norwich
(Dame Julian's Hazelnut)
(14ᵗʰ century)

When I saw the vision of his bleeding head, our Lord also showed my soul the unpretentious manner of his loving. I saw that for us he is everything that is good, comforting, and helpful. He is our clothing who wraps us up and holds us close for love. —Revelations of Divine Love
by Julian of Norwich, Chapter Five

When Julian of Norwich was thirty years old she was intensely sick and close to death. At this time she had a number of visions of Christ on the cross, the motherhood of God, and God's mercy for each and all of us. Julian recovered and lived many more years, writing down what she had learned.

And with this insight he also showed me a little thing, the size of a hazelnut, lying in the palm of my hand. It seemed to me as round as a ball. I gazed at it and thought, "What can this be?" The answer came thus, "It is everything that is made." I marveled how this could be, for it was so small it seemed it might fall suddenly into nothingness. Then I heard the answer, "It lasts, and ever shall last, because God loves it. All things have their being in this way by the grace of God."
—Revelations of Divine Love
by Julian of Norwich, Chapter Five

السَّلِيبِي الْقِدِّيس يُوحَنَّا

SAN IVAN DE LA CRVZ

Saint John of the Cross
(1542-1591)

As a child, John of the Cross grew up in extreme poverty in the slums where Islamic converts or their descendants lived in northern Spain. One of his brothers died of malnutrition, and John suffered from rickets, which kept him from growing any taller than five feet. The great mystical poetry he wrote as an adult was strongly influenced by the Moorish love ballads he heard throughout his youth.

After joining the Carmelite Order, he met Saint Teresa of Avila and became a part of her reform movement. He worked to reform his order for nine years, and was then arrested by Carmelites opposed to the reform and imprisoned for nine months in the tiny guest latrine of a friary in Toledo. The stench there made breathing difficult, and his body became infested with worms. He finally escaped at night through a window by climbing down a makeshift rope, but not before he had composed some of the world's most beautiful mystical poetry.

Working again among the reformed houses, he was eventually exiled to a remote friary when extremists opposed his more moderate position. There he soon became very sick, but was refused proper food and medical care by the local superior, who bore him a grudge. He died just before midnight December 14, 1591.

In this icon he holds a ball of flames. Flame also arises from his head, as a symbol of the divine love that filled his soul—love he described as living flames in his poetry. The inscription by his head is Arabic for Saint John of the Cross and honors the Arabic heritage he received from his mother. The inscription at the bottom is the same, but in Spanish, written in the old Latin letters that were in style in his day.

Ḣ ẤΓΆ ΒΡΊ ΓΙ ΔΑ

Ḣ ẤΓΆ ΔΑΡ ΛΥ ΔΆ ΧΑ

naoṁ bríd agus naoṁ ḋarluḋaċ

Saints Brigid and Darlughdach
(5th-6th centuries)

Together with many other peoples around the earth, the ancient Celts believed that mystery often reveals itself in the betwixt and between. On the banks of rivers and lakes, at the edge of fog, even on thresholds or at fences, one might suddenly glimpse what is really real, or even be caught out of oneself into the world of spirit.

Brigid and her dear friend and successor Darlughdach lived at the betwixt and between when Ireland was converting from its ancient faith to Christianity. What had been a druidic college became a convent of nuns, the chief druidess became an abbess who would become a major Irish saint. It was a time recorded in poetry and myth, a time when mystical Celtic Christianity was forged from what had been and what was to be.

We know that the new abbess Brigid presided over a double monastery of men and women, that the nuns continued to tend the perpetual fire that had burned there since druidic times, and that Brigid and her successors presided over the bishops of their region until the Synod of Kells in 1152. The sacred fire was only extinguished when Henry VIII drove the nuns out a thousand years later. It was relit in 1993 when two Brigidine nuns returned to live at Kildare.

The nuns wear white habits similar to their clothing as druidesses. They are tonsured in the Celtic style, from ear to ear forward. Since fire is the symbol of Sophia-Wisdom in the north, the fiery mandala contains a face of Christ from the Book of Kells. Sophia is the bond between them and the mistress-muse of all mystics. The three flames above their heads are a reminder that the pre-Christian Brigid had been a triple goddess, and that Celtic mysticism has always been trinitarian.

To be betwixt and between is to be on the margins. All mystics in every tradition have found themselves there. As Merton would say, it is only from the margin that one can see things in proper perspective, the perspective from which God sees things, the perspective of a child.

REFLECTION *by Edwina Gateley*

They are the meteors in our grey world—visionaries and mystics, who, at certain points in our human journey, burst forth with powerful spiritual insights that remind us, as we stumble on, that God is with us. This God shines through visionaries and mystics—transparent and deeply comforting. Particularly in times of oppression and struggle, such people—like lights in dark places—bring us new vision and hope that is often so radical and threatening to the status quo that the message is ignored, ridiculed, or downright repressed.

History reveals, however, that, ultimately, the spiritual power that marks and transforms the lives of these amazing individuals impacts all of us. Like it or not, believe it or not, God speaks through humanity and through all creation—and God's voice cannot be silenced. Like the tiny, persistent violet that grows beneath concrete blocks, seeking tiny cracks beneath the great repressive weight, the fragile yet powerful beauty of God's grace ultimately breaks through to leave us in wonderment.

The mystic does not have to be a religiously credentialed member of any priesthood or church hierarchy. God is essentially egalitarian in the person visited with mystical awareness. For that reason, too, the mystic can be a threat to established religious institutions and authorities; they are therefore often eager to crush the tiny violets. The mystics and visionaries, who have gone before us and those who live amongst us, are conduits of revelation and grace beyond the norm. They represent "God with us" in such an intense way that, when we open ourselves to the revelation they present, we are, ourselves, brought a little closer to the vision of God in our midst—particularly when we are desperately hungry for such a vision. God's voice breaks into our story in our most violent and fearful times—of war, oppression, disease and despair—and through that voice and those who express it, we know, for all the mess that we create, that God can never, will never, leave us orphans.

The mystical journey is a very individual one. There is no "right way" to be a mystic. John of the Cross, Julian of Norwich, Brigid of Kildare, and Black Elk each have a different story of their journey to God. For John of the Cross it was torturous, as his witness to the dark night of the soul attests. For Julian, the fullness of God was revealed in a hazelnut along with a profound and comforting awareness that "All shall be well." Brigid brought to bear on her community the maternal, feminine face of God. And Black Elk's vision was given to him as a child and returned to him in old age. Yet all of them lived in times of oppression, internalizing the pain, suffering, desolation, and societal chaos of their time—yet emerging transformed, with visions of splendor and wonder.

Despite the uniqueness of their spiritual journeys, all mystics remind us of the eternal truth that pain and suffering are essential ingredients of the journey, stripping us of ego and the self-delusion that we are in charge and in control. Such a stripping clears the way for a vision of God—a glimpse of the divine at our deep center. What the mystics and visionaries experienced externally in their struggles with the reality of oppression around them, reflects the internal spiritual struggle to which all who seek wholeness are called. It is a long, hard journey, often abandoned in despair and disillusionment. The experiences of resilient souls like John of the Cross stand as a beacon for us, proclaiming that the human spirit, charged with divine grace, is eminently capable of shining even in the deepest darkness. That very shining tells us, with incisive clarity, that God is here and we tread on sacred ground. Such is the ground of the visionaries and mystics. Thus these great souls are gifts in our lives—signs too, of God's great compassion for us, showing us the way when we can barely see.

The great mystics and visionaries stand as monumental and historically significant revelations of God at particular points in human history. But, in addition, they invite all of us to dare to be open to transformation through the Holy Spirit—Sophia Wisdom—who, according to biblical tradition, is the revelation of God and God's Co-Creative Partner. It is she who invites us to be mystics. If we dare listen, and dare be open to a deeper way of living and being by becoming conscious of our connectedness to all living things, we begin to experience the mystery of God's presence. It is that presence which overwhelms mystics and visionaries as they become conscious of all things as being charged with divine grace. Everywhere is holy ground. Any one of us can walk upon that holy ground if we allow ourselves to be open.

I know something about that. For me the streets of Chicago, which I was called to walk, became holy ground. However, in response to this call to minister with women in prostitution, I was frequently terrified. I was always vulnerable. But I carried within me a deep and profound certainty that flowed from a personal mystical experience that God had called me to be on those streets. For me, regardless of perceived or imagined danger or risk, I knew without a doubt that I had to follow that call. It was simply greater than any fear or obstacle before me. I was also driven by an overwhelming sense of compassion that, in reflection, I know to be God. The mystical experience, beyond any human rationalization, drives one into strange and awesome places. No matter how cold or grey or forbidding the space, it is the territory of the Holy Spirit. In this process of revelation, trust and vulnerability are prerequisite.

So it was that when I came to a run-down tavern on the corner of a dark alley, I knew without a doubt that I had to go in, that that was where I was supposed to be. Inside it was dark—but I could feel the bodies jostling around the bar counter. I felt utterly alone in that dirty place and yet, paradoxically, utterly at home, simply because it was the right place for me to be at that time. It is amazing the grace that becomes available to us when we follow the deep truth (God) within us. We dare tread in unknown places when, for whatever mysterious reason, we believe God walks before us making all space holy.

As I sat on a bar stool in the dim light late that night, a woman in her mid-fifties shuffled up to the bar and struggled onto the stool next to me. Banging her fist on the counter she demanded a "jug o' wine" from the bar man. Eventually she glanced at me. "You hungry?" she demanded.

Anxious to be receptive, I replied that, yes, I was—a little.

With great satisfaction the woman bent down and pulled a loaf of white sliced bread from her plastic bag on the ground. "Good," she proclaimed, "I ain't eaten for three days and I just stole this loaf o' bread from the supermarket down the street and I was looking for someone to share it with."

I stared in amazement. But more surprises were to come. After opening the loaf and taking out a couple of slices of bread, she bent down again and from her bag she produced, triumphantly, an open can of tuna fish wrapped in plastic. She then proceeded to scoop out the tuna with her hand and spread it on the bread—producing a soggy sandwich that she then offered to me with a great smile: "Here you are, honey," she declared. Having safely deposited the sandwich in my hands, she then proceeded to fill up my then-empty glass from her "jug." I found myself in one of those unreal situations that somehow impel you, nevertheless, to participate. As I looked at my new-

found companion I experienced a stirring of compassion from somewhere quite deep in me. This woman, for all her strange behavior, was my sister.

As I tentatively ate and drank, the woman talked—or, rather, rambled, something to the effect of it being a hard life and how it was a struggle to get by and to survive. She lamented that she could only "pick up $5 or $10 a day" and that she did not know what she was going to do. Tears began to roll down her face as she looked at me again . . . and then again. Suddenly it seemed as if she had an inspiration, for she grabbed at my arm as she looked me up and down and then blurted out: "Oh, honey, I know where the tricks are. With my experience and your body, we could work together—we could be a team . . ." Then I realized, to my horror, that this woman was an older prostitute and that times were hard for her now—and she was asking ME to team up with her! Almost apologetically I explained that I was not involved in prostitution.

"What are you doing here, then?" she demanded. "This is a hooker bar—this is where the guys come to pick up a girl. Who are you?"

I stumbled my words: "I'm a Christian . . . I'm a . . . an independent Catholic minister . . ."

"A what?" she cried out in disbelief. "Ain't never been no minister in 'ere before. This ain't no place for no minister—ain't no place for no Christian. You shouldn't be here . . . ain't no place for people like you . . ." The presence of someone who simply believed in God and claimed it triggered an emotional response in my new-found companion. She began to weep steadily as she told me her life story—of how, after years of incest and abuse as a child she ran away from home when she was a teenager, was soon picked up by a pimp on the streets, introduced to drugs, and soon primed for a life of prostitution. It was all she had ever done. And now she was too old for it all and moving rapidly into the lifestyle of a bag lady. Now she was totally alone and desperate. All I could do in that bar that night was hold that broken woman who had told her story of violence and poverty to a stranger. And so we clung together in that dirty place— two women weeping and looking for a dream.

Early the following morning I left the bar feeling all emptied out and helpless. The woman with whom I had spent the last three hours lay huddled in a corner fast asleep—her face still damp with tears. Walking home in the greasy darkness of wet streets, I reflected on what had happened. As I did so, it was as if a blindfold suddenly slipped from my eyes and I pierced the veil from ordinary consciousness to a deeper place: I had gone into the bar—vulnerable, open, and looking for God. And this woman had come into the dark place in which I had found myself. She brought the bread— and she broke it and shared it with me. She brought the fish and she shared it with me. Then she took the wine and she shared that with me too. And then she told me her story and she embraced me. Then I knew. I knew with a deep and transforming insight that there had been, in that dirty place that night, a eucharist, and that the Holy Spirit— Wisdom—ever elusive, ever roaming free, had been present in the coming together of open hearts seeking compassion and grasping at connections right in the heart of brokenness

and vulnerability. God did not need a church or recognized holy places to be present. Rather, the ordinary place, two women, stolen bread, cheap wine, and fish became the place of mystical encounter.

For me, this was a mystical experience, an experience of one-ness in God and of the mystery of God's presence totally gratuitous, breaking through in a moment of faith. As such it is an invitation to a divine rendezvous. When such invitations impel us to open our hearts and our arms, we cannot but be overwhelmed. We cannot but be amazed at God— with us and in us. We cannot but be deeply grateful to sink, even for a moment, into the vision of God. For mysticism is about moments of pure bliss when we are bathed in God.

Ah, these mystics and these visionaries!
Sick or imprisoned,
crushed down or broken up—
they stand before us
astounded recipients of God's glance
penetrating human blindness,
amazed themselves and humbled
at the wonders wrought in them.
For they see the purple hills
behind the prison bars,
and they know that there is healing
within the sickened soul.
Even beyond the broken bodies,
in the heart of stolen land,
they proclaim our call to freedom
in the shining of their eyes.
Ah, these mystics and these visionaries!
Radiant as the sun—
they rise from their frail humanity,
all awash with grace and mystery
to tell us who we are.

By God's free Spirit seized,
they whisper of the fire
that burns through all
our small vain ways,
leaving only brilliant Essence,
a startling, holy Beauty

in the stillpoint of our souls.
Ah, these mystics and these visionaries!
Who visit us with glory
and leave us standing, trembling,
at their rendezvous with God.

The Artist, the Poet, and the Child

At this time the disciples came to Jesus and said, "Who is the greatest in the Kingdom of heaven?" So he called a little child to him and set the child in front of them. Then he said, "I tell you solemnly, unless you change and become like little children you will never enter the Kingdom of heaven. And so, the one who becomes as little as this little child is the greatest in the Kingdom of heaven."

—Matthew 18:1-4

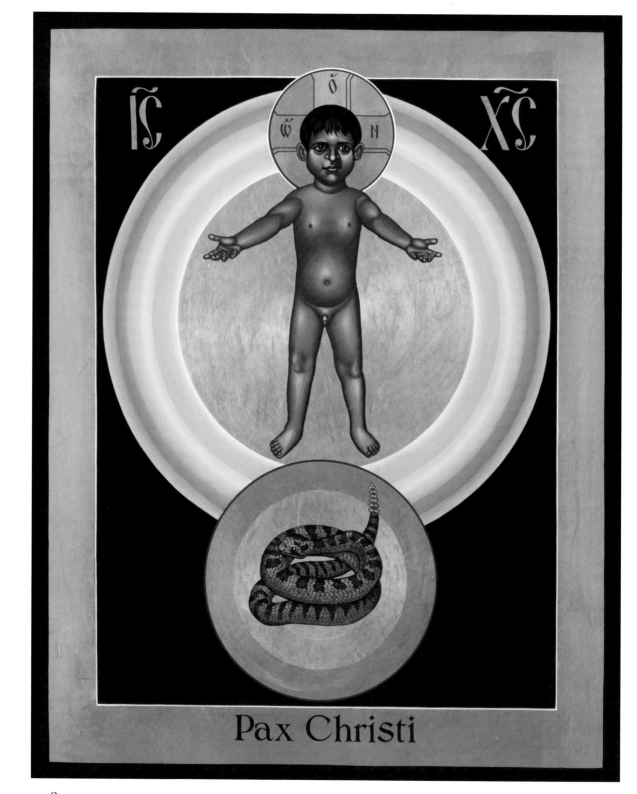

Pax Christi

Pax Christi

Religions inspire humankind in its pursuit of elusive ideals. They do this by providing systems of myths and symbols. These myths and symbols are poetic and are not usually meant to be taken literally. They beckon cultures forward to higher moral accomplishments and challenge individuals to greater personal growth.

Peace has been an elusive ideal for most of human history. Christians and Jews find inspiration in their pursuit of this ideal in the imagery surrounding their promised messiah. Throughout their sacred scriptures, the coming of the messiah is described in terms of a reign of peace. Perhaps the most beautiful description is in the prophecies of Isaiah 11, where the messiah is a tiny child surrounded by traditional enemies who now live together in peace. The child messiah plays over the viper's den, and none of the animals do harm to one another.

This icon depicts the vision of Isaiah. A peaceful Christ child stands above a coiled rattlesnake. Both are surrounded by mandalas of light to emphasize that the snake, too, is holy—that being powerfully dangerous does not make it evil. The child is comfortable in his nakedness, inviting humankind to make peace with our own bodies. Shame leads to violence, and countless millions feel shame toward their very selves. A rainbow surrounds the mandala of the Christ, a reminder of the sign of peace given to Noah in another beautiful biblical myth. The inscription at the bottom is Latin for "Peace of Christ."

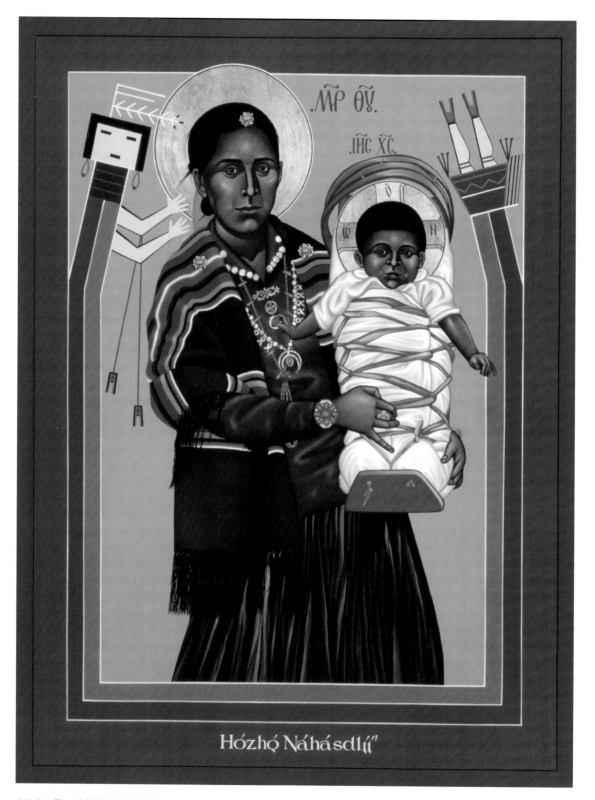

Hózhǫ́ Náhásdlį́į́"

Navaho Madonna

In New Mexico and Arizona, the Navaho people preserve an ancient way of life on a remnant of what was once their land. This icon celebrates the beauty of Navaho culture and its closeness to the Christian Gospel.

Beauty—*hozho*—is the highest Navaho ideal. Most Navahos are artists of some sort, and their spirituality is woven around beauty. Beauty includes harmony, goodness, well-being, and order. Sickness and other ills come when humans do not live in a beautiful manner. The Navaho phrase at the bottom of the icon is repeated four times at the end of their religious ceremonies: "Beauty has been re-established." This is also the message of Christ's incarnation.

Mary here wears her traditional Byzantine colors, but she is a Navaho woman. Jesus is strapped to a cradleboard and he is laughing for his first time—a special moment in every Navaho's life. His parents will now give a feast so that he will not be stingy as he grows up. The inscription by Mary's head is Church Slavonic for "Mother of God." The inscription above the cradleboard is "Jesus Christ," and the letters in Christ's halo mean "I am who am," the name God told to Moses in the Old Testament. Around the bottom and sides of the icon is one of the Holy People of Navaho religion—a Rainbow Yei. He always surrounds religious sand paintings.

Childlike laughter and beauty are two ways Navaho culture can enrich traditional Christian spirituality. The world is a divine epiphany, if only we had eyes to see. After viewing this world as a place of exile, let us listen to what the Holy Spirit speaks to us from the Navaho culture:

> *In Beauty (happily) I walk*
> *With Beauty before me I walk*
> *With Beauty behind me I walk*
> *With Beauty above me I walk*
> *With Beauty all around me I walk*
> *It is finished in Beauty.* —Yeibichai Chant

Ὁ ἅγιος Ἰωάννης

JOHANN SEBASTIAN BACH

Johann Sebastian Bach
(1685-1750)

Johann Sebastian Bach is one of the greatest composers in the history of western music. His work has nourished the spiritual lives of millions, regardless of culture, language, or creed. He has been called the "Fifth Evangelist," so effectively has he proclaimed the mystery of Christ in the language of art. A devout Lutheran, he represents the mystical side of Protestantism—those who move beyond moral teachings and the printed word to encounter the living Word, face-to-face.

Bach was born into a musical family, and was taught violin and organ as a child. He was orphaned at nine years old. By the age of eighteen, he had already begun his professional life. More than 1,000 of his musical compositions survive, including works in every musical form of his day, except opera. He wrote five sets of religious cantatas for every Sunday and feast day of the church year. He taught music, directed choirs, played the organ for services, and was a devoted father to his many children. He enjoyed the pleasures of the flesh, including a glass of good wine and his tobacco pipe. When asked how he had achieved so much, his reply was, "I have had to be industrious."

Bach was not a self-consciously pious man, but his entire life was focused on the Divine Mystery. He began his manuscripts "in the Name of Jesus." He felt that "the aim and final reason . . . of all music . . . should be none else but the Glory of God and the recreation of the mind." Blessed with the vision of what he was meant to do, he followed his aims tenaciously and fought all interference. That sometimes led to difficulties with his employers, something many artists have had to endure. Two and a half centuries after his death, however, his music continues to bring souls to God—living proof of the rightness of his path.

J.R.R. TOLKIEN

J. R. R. TOLKIEN
(1892-1973)

John Ronald Reuel Tolkien is one of the world's great storytellers. He lost both his parents by the time he was twelve. A priest of the Birmingham Oratory then took him under his wing and saw to his education. Though his early years had been spent in rural settings, as an orphan he was forced to live in crowded cities. From childhood he had been fascinated by languages, mostly for their beautiful sounds. Surrounded by urban squalor, he took refuge in his imagination and began inventing new languages.

Soon after his marriage, he was sent to fight in France during World War I and contracted trench fever. After convalescing in England, he taught languages at Oxford most of the rest of his life. As a scholar he lived at the margin of society, nourishing society by his teaching and research. He died in a rest home at the age of eighty-one.

He is best known as the author of *The Hobbit* and *The Lord of the Rings*, stories that began as entertainment for his two young sons, but that developed into a vast work of mythology. Starting with languages he invented, he imagined races of people to speak the languages, then histories and mythologies for the peoples, and finally geographies in which the histories and mythologies could take place. As a devout Catholic intellectual, he felt that such creative use of our imagination was a reflection of God's own creative activity, God in whose image we are made. Like an alchemist, he transformed his experiences and suffering at life's margins into timeless truths that rise to the level of myth. Millions have read his books, which have now been translated into many different languages, and have rediscovered in themselves the childlike gift of imagination that belongs to us all as icons of God.

ἡ ἁγία ΘΕΡΕΣΙΑ

Saint Thérèse of Lisieux
(1873-1897)

Until recent times it was difficult to find a Catholic church without a statue of Thérèse of the Infant Jesus. While statues seem less in vogue since Vatican II, this saint remains one of the most popular in the Roman Church. On one level she accomplished next-to-nothing in her brief life. When she died of tuberculosis at the age of twenty-four, the prioress of her monastery wondered what she could possibly write in the obituary that would be sent to the other Carmelite monasteries. On a deeper level Thérèse helped revolutionize modern Christian concepts of holiness.

She came from a bourgeois family and was a spoiled child. When two of her older sisters entered the local Carmelite monastery, she made up her mind to follow them. She received special permission to enter monastic life when she was only fifteen. Her remaining nine years were spent washing laundry, sweeping corridors, and struggling to stay awake during meditation. After developing tuberculosis, she was appointed mistress of novices. The superior of the monastery also ordered her to write an account of her life, which has become one of the most widely read books on spirituality in modern times.

Thérèse described her vocation as simply loving. Whereas many Christians had often suspected that being holy meant only something dramatic—being eaten by lions, sitting for fifty years on top of a pillar, whipping oneself daily—Thérèse believed that doing one's ordinary work was quite enough, provided all was done with love. She strove in every way to identify herself with the people of her time. On a deeper plane this sharing was manifested in spiritual suffering, when she lost all sense of God's presence in her life during her last few years. She continued to embrace everything with generous love, including her fatal illness, in spite of the spiritual aridity that she felt. This darkness and aridity finally lifted in her last few minutes, and she died in ecstasy. She is depicted with roses as a symbol of the prayers she promised after her death.

Children live at the margins of the adult world and can usually hardly wait for the day that world becomes theirs. They lose much, however, when they pass from childhood. Spiritual realities seem ever more remote and sometimes are forgotten completely. While Thérèse stopped being a spoiled child her soul never ceased being child-like. She reminds us of the paradox that the path to spiritual maturity, the way into God's Kingdom, is to become again as children. She inspires us to recover the spiritual treasures we may have lost on our rush to adulthood: imagination, simplicity, playfulness, and awe.

REFLECTION *by Edwina Gateley*

We are, apparently, the hardest working industrialized nation in the world with the longest number of working hours a year, but the least vacation time. We are, consequently, the most productive nation and one of the wealthiest. But at what cost! The reality is—we are exhausted!

In our relentless pursuit of the work ethic we have left behind a great deal of value—time to play, time to pray, and time to be creative and imaginative. We have, effectively, abandoned an essential part of our humanity and, in the process, we have almost lost touch with the incredible dimension of the human spirit—our creative imagination—that leads us to a deeper and richer life through the gifts of co-creation. The roles of the artist, the poet, and the child in presenting us with a different and more holistic perspective on life have been marginalized in a society frantically caught up in the pursuit of success, security, and money. But no matter how fast we travel or how high we climb, there will always be within us a hunger for that which we leave behind in the race to get ahead. We are left bereft, and we sicken. For even as we go about our frenetic business, there is a child in us who longs to play and an artist who can, but dares not, paint. Music is locked away in our hearts and there is a poem waiting to be spoken in our souls.

A culture that has lost touch with its creative soul looks in a different direction for solace and comfort, towards anything that will help us feel better or anesthetize our pain. We become an addictive society seeking satisfaction from potions, pills, and possessions instead of fulfillment from within. The government constantly threatens to cut off support for the arts, believing that other priorities demand its attention. In both body and soul the artists of our culture face starvation.

But there are moments when we become acutely conscious of our hunger for beauty, art, or play. These may be times when—in a moment of solitude—we hear the song of a bird or the wash of the ocean on the shore; or we may be touched by a thing of beauty, or a poem, prayer, or song. We hear the haunting rich beauty of the music of Bach composed from a heart bursting with grace. Fleetingly, we experience a different level of awareness. We know we are graced and we know we are gifted. We know with our hearts that we rest in a different dimension of reality.

There are also those in our world whose songs, words, or creative gifts are so rich and universal that when we experience them a longing stirs, oh, so deep within us, reminding us of the truth we may have forgotten and the hunger we have not fed. Such has been the music and artistry of the Navaho culture, a solace to the marginal and a threat to the powerful. It is not unusual that in a repressive system the voice of the artist rises—articulating the unrealized dreams and longings in peoples' hearts and often reminding them of their communal strength. (The songs the Africans sang while enslaved were a source of enormous inspiration and comfort when they had little else to hold onto. It was through song and story that much of their African culture and tradition was nourished and passed on.)

The artist reminds us of our repressed hunger for beauty by presenting images and sounds, which connect us to the source of that hunger in our souls. Beauty has the inherent power to enrich and nourish all of us—effectively to feed and heal our inner selves. Starvation—rampant in our world—is not only of the physical kind, but is also spiritual when our inner selves are starved of creativity, art, and beauty. Most of us are aware of how we can be touched or moved by a beautiful sunset or a splendid view. The English poet William Wordsworth writes of how beauty was a constant source of nourishment to him:

These beauteous forms,
Through a long absence, have not been to me
As is a landscape to a blind man's eye:
But oft, in lonely rooms, and 'mid the din
Of towns and cities, I have owed to them
In hours of weariness, sensations sweet,
And passing even into my purer mind
With tranquil restoration . . .

—LINES COMPOSED A FEW MILES
ABOVE TINTERN ABBEY

The healing and nourishing power of beauty—whether in the form of music, poetry, or art—cannot be underestimated, particularly in our fast-moving and achievement-oriented society. Someone once said that we are forever changed when we stand and gaze at the moon . . . We slip into a deeper place . . . a place of vision, beauty, and imagination, such as the writings of J. R. R. Tolkien invite us into, reminding us of the creative presence of Sophia Wisdom—reminding us all of the power of beauty and its capacity to transport us into a deeper awareness.

Once I took an elderly "bag lady" from the city streets for a day trip to the countryside. We walked through a forest and came to a running stream. I shall never forget the look of awe and delight on her face as she stared, mesmerized, at the clear, bubbling stream: "Ain't never seen no stream before," she whispered. "Ain't it beautiful."

As we moved on in silence I saw her wiping tears from her eyes. Her whole being, starved of inspiration on the drab streets where she spent her life, had been moved by a vision of beauty. And she would never be quite the same again. I prayed that, like Wordsworth, she would remember the lovely place she had seen and that the memory would give to her "In hours of weariness, sensations sweet . . ." As she slept in shelters or alleys I hoped that she would hear, in her loneliness, the comforting lullaby of the running stream.

When I opened a house for women recovering from prostitution and drugs in the city, it was a priority for me to create an environment of beauty for these most broken women. I insisted that they deserved the best, that—given their years of exposure to violence, poverty, and ugliness—their souls were thirsting for beauty and for healing. So I decorated the house as tastefully as I knew how and ensured that there were lots of plants around and fresh, bright flowers on the table. I also hung works of art on the walls and put pieces of pottery on display. The effect on the women was tangible. They often told me how their environment of beauty made them feel honored and good about themselves. Beauty is a natural healer. Whilst the creative arts are not a priority in our culture we will be bereft and underfed. We would do well, indeed, to learn from the Navaho whose culture gives central place to beauty and its expression in art.

Biblically, also, we are reminded of the sacredness of creativity. In the Book of Proverbs the Holy Spirit is depicted as Co-Creator with Yahweh:

> . . . *when he laid down the foundations of the*
> *earth,*
> *I was by his side, a master artist,*
> *delighting him day after day, ever at play in*
> *his presence,*
> *at play everywhere in the world . . .*
> —PROVERBS 8:29-31

The Holy Spirit is playful and elusive. Birther of new things, she is the one who will surprise us with possibilities if we are open to her. It is Sophia Wisdom who will lead the child in us and teach us how compassionate is the face of God—seducing us to quiet and lonely places to be still and to listen that we might be healed of our exhaustion. It is she who is the stillpoint in our souls. It is she who will lead us to the Christ Child of Peace. When we dare let go of our desire for success and security, and spend, instead, time alone to nurture our inner life, we will begin to enter the realm of the poet, the artist, and the child. She will lead us on that journey if our hearts are open. We will be surprised at what she will teach us. I was, when I met and came to know Stella.

Stella came to personify for me the true and full meaning of the words from Isaiah "And a little child shall lead them" (Isaiah:11:6). Like Thérèse of Lisieux, Stella, so open and so trusting, revealed to me the joy of the child, the beauty of simplicity. She was so tiny I nearly missed her. Rolled up tightly on the steps of the church, she huddled against the midnight chill. But from my sidelong glance I caught the shiver running along her shoulders and knew I must stop—reluctantly—for who knew what might be the consequences of such a late night encounter?

Her name was Stella and she was terrified. Even so, she accepted my invitation to come home with me where I would give her a bed and something to eat. Along with Stella came her garbage—two huge plastic bags filled with whatever the streets and alleys had offered on her long, shuffling journeys. I was disturbed by the garbage. Concerned about bugs and cockroaches and smells. But Stella clutched her plastic bags fiercely and with a dignity that surprised me. Grey haired, bowlegged, and only four feet in height, the little old lady ambled innocently after me dragging her garbage.

For three months we lived together, Stella, myself, and the garbage. Every day she would go off to the streets and return with more. As she lovingly stuffed it under the bed and in the closet, her faded blue eyes twinkled and shone with triumph and delight. At last she had a storage place for the only possessions she had. By virtue of that very fact, the garbage was, in a very real sense, precious. I was deeply humbled as I reflected on this. Who was I to despise and dismiss so easily the treasures of another?

On one occasion Stella came with me to a barbecue and was presented with two hamburgers. Seconds later they were gone. "Did you eat those already?" I asked in disbelief. Stella mumbled and turned away, clutching her plate of french fries. Then I saw the bulge like hamburgers in her pockets—round and seeping grease. "Stella, you don't need to hide them. There'll be more if you need," I protested. Her eyes held mine and I saw in them a deep fear reflecting years of hunger and poverty and the indignity of scavenging for food . . . "Let me put them in a bag for you." It was I who mumbled. How could I even begin to understand the insecurity of an old lady living on the streets?

Stella was very amusing. So delighted was she to be loved, she frequently assailed me with witty remarks and jokes, which she followed with bursts of giggles. She was extremely funny. (She could have been an actress . . . a comedian . . . a college professor . . .) But she was a bag lady—a gentle, timid bag lady who now followed me around like a puppy dog and told me jokes to make me happy.

Eventually I found a place for Stella in a home for the elderly. She hated the transition, but I knew she would be well cared for and have more company. I assured her I would visit often and we would spend vacation time together.

Stella received around $20 a month for herself. And every month she sent me half of this small allowance: "For the girls on the streets," she wrote on a scrap of paper enclosing the $10 bill. It was, indeed, the widow's mite.

I visited Stella whenever I could and took her for little trips. It did not take much to make her happy. A trip out for a hot dog and ice cream; a game of bingo; an evening spent sitting around the kitchen table telling stories. Stella delighted in all small things. One day she told me a secret: "My name," she whispered, "is not Stella . . . I am Sophia."

I bought Sophia a polyester red jacket, second hand, from the Goodwill Store. She loved it. So much in fact that she refused to take it off (except in bed and to be laundered). She wore her red jacket every day until she died eight years later. When Sophia lay dying in the hospital, all shriveled up, with wrinkled skin soft as a newborn, I held her hand. She could not speak but she stared at me with those still twinkling, fast fading eyes. "I love you, Sophia," I whispered.

Sophia, wanderer of the streets and alleys, Sophia, who came so unexpectedly into my life, Sophia, teacher of wisdom and simplicity, Sophia—I love you.

Sophia slipped away from me.

And I wept.

> Starved for loveliness
> she stood,
> stunned,
> by the little stream

that ran
so free and clear and carefree
before her weary eyes—
now widening—
incredulous
at the vision.
I stood apart
from the encounter
suddenly humbled—
aware of sacredness
in the revelation of beauty
before eyes
accustomed only
to the grime of city streets,
and the grey dying
of the hopeless and abandoned.
As if to anchor
the moment,
she dug deep
into the pockets
of her shabby coat—
stuffed with old tissues
and free candy—

and, rooting herself hungrily
in the moist earth,
she whispered:
"Ain't it beautiful."
(Hushed tones
claiming and consecrating
sacred ground.)

The Universe stilled
before her bowed head
as Artist, Poet, and Child—
so long dead
in dried-up womb—
quickened
at the threads of life
stirring in her belly—
unleashing tears,
deep and fresh,
to run with the stream—
playful and joyous—
to a place
of endless freedom.

Epilogue

More than forty of my icons are scattered through this book. Like all icons, they are windows to the world of spirit. In style they resemble icons found on Mount Athos, in Greece. In content they are often revolutionary.

People often ask me how I began painting icons of modern "saints." My father's family came from tsarist Russia. We are of Cossack stock, having Muslim and Christian "blood" mixed together in our souls. I am a Byzantine iconographer trained in the strictest of Orthodox schools. I spent the first eighteen years of my adult life in Catholic and Orthodox monasteries. How is it that I now live at the margins of that world, painting icons that are so different from those of my peers? I hope you saw the answer in the pages of this book, but here is a little bit of background.

To belong to an immigrant family in America, with roots in different religious traditions has always left me feeling a bit of a pilgrim. I grew up on tales of saints and labor unions the way other children grow up with fairy tales. My Russian grandmother was there with images of saints covering her living room walls. She taught me that religion was life, not an isolated element in my life. Her eyes reflected her faith. She found God wherever she looked.

My father was also there, telling me Gospel stories, like the one about Lazarus and the rich man, and about children a little older than me who had worked and died in mines and factories in this country. I knew about the Ludlow massacre that happened south of where we lived in Colorado, where company goons had killed men, women, and children on a cold Easter morning in 1914. We made pilgrimages to Wounded Knee and Sand Creek. I learned the darker side of American history.

Grandma showed me a transcendent, infinite God, and icons that spoke eloquently of that God. My father showed me a human Christ, still suffering in our midst and asking us to respond. These memories haunted me all the years I lived in monasteries. When I left in 1982 and began painting icons fulltime in San Francisco, it was only a few months before these two themes began to intertwine in my work.

San Francisco itself was an education for me. From the peace of cloistered life, I was suddenly thrown into a political maelstrom where I encountered for the first time communists, anarchists, feminists, gay men and women, undocumented aliens, and many others whose life experiences had been so different from my own. After initial fear and shock, I slowly learned to listen. Despite dissimilar trappings, I discovered we had more in common than not. The face of Christ began to emerge for me there at the margins of all I had previously known.

It has never been my way to seek change for its own sake. I am a conservative at heart, with a great love for tradition. Perhaps it is precisely my love for tradition that recognizes that it must evolve if it is not to become obsolete and die. Change seldom occurs at the center, but works its way inward from the margins. On the streets of San Francisco I embraced the margins as an iconographer, ready to wrestle with whatever changes would be demanded from me as a result. The rest is history.

Like Edwina Gateley, I am comfortable living in the margins. Like her, I have been misunderstood but I continue forward, no matter how lonely the path sometimes seems. I am deeply honored to be able to join forces with Edwina to produce this book. It is a work of love that we present to the world with love.

–Robert Lentz